Meditation
A Practical Guidebook

SWAMI TADATMANANDA

Meditation
A Practical Guidebook

Based on the Teachings of
Vedanta, Bhagavad Gita & Yoga Sutras

New Age Books

New Delhi (India)

MEDITATION: A PRACTICAL GUIDEBOOK

ISBN: 978-81-7822-424-4
First NAB Edition: Delhi, 2014

Published by
NEW AGE BOOKS
A-44 Naraina Industrial Area, Phase-I
New Delhi (India)-110 028
E-mail: nab@newagebooksindia.com
Website: www.newagebooksindia.com

> **NAB Cataloging-in-Publication Data**
> MEDITATION: A JOURNEY OF EXPLORATION
> ISBN 978-81-7822-424-4
> (Index, Preface, Introduction, Appendics)

Printed and published by
RP Jain for NAB Printing Unit
A-44, Naraina Industrial Area
Phase-I, New Delhi-110 028. India

ACKNOWLEDGEMENTS

First and foremost, I wish to acknowledge my guru, Pujya Swami Dayananda Saraswati, whose masterful teaching of Vedanta and meditation opened my eyes to the wisdom of the ancient *rishis*. His guidance set me rightly on a profound, lifelong journey of spiritual growth.

I want to thank several of my students who were instrumental in preparing this book. Joseph Sundwal provided artwork and editorial advice. Mala Balasubramaniam, Chandrakala Kamath, Kishin Kripalani, and Neelu Reddy helped with proofreading. Anju Makhijani made the arrangements to have this book printed.

Finally, I thank all those who have attended my programs at Arsha Bodha Center and elsewhere over the years. Their dedication and thirst for spiritual wisdom has been a constant source of inspiration.

CONTENTS

INDEX TO
MEDITATION EXERCISES

Note on Sanskrit Usage

To assist those unable to read the *Devanāgarī* script, all Sanskrit words have been transliterated using Roman letters. The International Alphabet of Sanskrit Transliteration (IAST) uses a large number of diacritical marks which may confuse non-academic readers. Therefore, I have adopted a simplified scheme of transliteration that uses a minimum of diacritics.

Guide to Pronunciation

a	agenda	t	top
ā	father	th	anthill
i	pit	d	did
ī	pizza	dh	madhouse
u	put	n	next
ū	rule		
e	prey	p	put
ai	aisle	ph	uphill
o	go	b	but
au	sauerkraut	bh	abhor
		m	mix
k	skate		
kh	blockhead	y	yes
g	good	r	drama
gh	log hut	l	lake
		v	van
c	church		
ch	beach house	sh	shine
j	just	s	sun
jh	hedge hog	h	hit

PREFACE

This book provides practical, methodical guidance for all who want to develop a powerful and rewarding practice of meditation. It begins with basic principles and proceeds step by step to more advanced topics while exploring a wide range of meditation techniques.

Though the subject is vast, I have tried to create a concise and user-friendly guidebook. This is exactly the kind of book I had hoped to find thirty years ago when my own meditation practice was in its infancy. Unfortunately, the books available then failed to satisfy my needs. Even today, such resources seem scarce.

I hope this book serves well as a guide and helpful companion for meditators on their journeys of spiritual growth.

Swami Tadatmananda
Arsha Bodha Center
Somerset, New Jersey
October, 2011

INTRODUCTION

To ask, "What is meditation?" is like asking, "What is music?" No simple answer can even hope to convey the breadth and richness of this subject. Meditation is a contemplative art, a mental discipline, and a sacred journey. Meditation is a reflective practice, a tranquil retreat, and a joyous excursion. Meditation is simultaneously an aesthetic pursuit, a scientific investigation, and a spiritual path. You could say that meditation is a rainbow of many hues.

But to describe meditation with fancy words and elegant expressions is like trying to describe the flavor of a ripe peach. Meditation, like the peach, must be experienced to be understood. Words can never suffice. Yet words of description and explanation are not useless. Words can tell you how to select the ripest fruit from a bushel of peaches. And words can tell you how to meditate, leading you to develop a powerful, rewarding practice.

Meditation has been practiced for millennia by Hindus and Buddhists, by Christians, Muslims and Jews, by followers of all the world's religious faiths and spiritual traditions. But it would be wrong to assume that meditation is meant only for those who live in monasteries, ashrams, or Himalayan caves. Meditation is valuable for people of all walks of life, as I discovered more than thirty years ago. Allow me to share with you a personal anecdote about how I came to discover the value of meditation.

In the late 1970's, I lived in California and worked as a computer engineer. In those days, the first wave of swamis and yogis from India had just begun to arrive in the U.S. Many landed on the shores of sunny California. I was to benefit immensely from this unique Indian import.

Though raised in a Christian family, I had long ago abandoned the religion of my childhood. Like many of my young American peers raised in the 1960's, I was interested in exploring Eastern Spirituality, as we called it. I was fortunate to have the opportunity to learn yoga and meditation from several swamis and their disciples.

My practice back then was rudimentary: a few yoga postures, some yogic breathing exercises, and several simple meditation techniques. In spite of being a complete novice, the benefits of my modest practice became apparent in a most unexpected context — at work.

I regularly attended meetings with managers and engineers who were predominately male, highly-opinionated, and assertive to the point of being aggressive. Impassioned arguments and loud voices were commonplace. But I sat quietly in those meetings, listening attentively while reviewing documents and making calculations. Our department manager took note of my silence and began to ask for my opinions. Soon, he regularly sought out and trusted my observations, perhaps because they seemed more objective than the brash assertions of others.

Before learning to meditate, I used to argue just as stridently as the others. Surprisingly, my meager practice had brought about immediate, helpful changes in my thinking and behavior. If a little meditation could be so beneficial, I realized that developing my practice could help me much more.

Meditation was the starting point for my journey of spiritual growth. That journey led me from guru to guru and from one spiritual tradition to another for several years. Then in 1981, I met the renowned traditional teacher of Vedanta, Swami Dayananda. Under his guidance, my spiritual pursuits flourished. I learned Sanskrit and studied Vedantic scriptures while living in his ashrams in India and the U.S. Eventually, I was initiated by him as a *sannyāsī*, a Hindu monk, on the banks of the Ganges River in 1993. Much more about my spiritual journey and my guru can be found in "Roar of the Ganges," a book I wrote soon after my initiation.

It is really not so strange that an American computer engineer would become a Hindu spiritual teacher. Like everyone, I pursued those things in life that seemed most valuable. In the practice of meditation and in the teachings of Vedanta, I found such extraordinary benefit that it was natural for me to devote my life to these sacred traditions. After three decades of personal practice and more than twenty years of public teaching, my appreciation has grown even deeper. Feeling the responsibility to share with others what I have learned, I set myself to the task of writing this book.

What Meditation is Not

There are many misconceptions about meditation. Wrong notions and false assumptions can get in the way of understanding the topics covered in this book. So before proceeding, let us identify and dismiss the most troublesome misconceptions.

Many believe that meditation is simply emptying your mind, leaving it vacant, blank, silent. But in the coming chapters, you will learn meditation techniques that engage your mind in activities like observing your thoughts or reciting a mantra. During such techniques, your mind cannot remain silent. So meditation is not merely making your mind blank.

Some believe that meditation is for experiencing bliss. It is true that when your mind becomes silent, bliss is indeed experienced. You confirm this every night in deep, dreamless sleep when you enjoy blissful slumber. So to experience bliss, you need not meditate; you can simply go to bed. But there is much more to meditation than merely enjoying a few moments of bliss.

Some say that meditation is a mystical condition or a state of superconsciousness. Lofty words like these can make meditation seem exotic and appealing. Yet such terms are not particularly helpful. The word mystical denotes an experience that defies explanation, an experience that cannot be understood or shared with others. If meditation were truly mystical, it could not be taught or learned. Further, the word superconsciousness is not found in any Hindu scripture; it seems to be an entirely modern concept. Words like these seem to promote or glorify meditation rather than provide genuine instruction.

Some criticize meditation, considering it an attempt to escape the troubles of life by shutting out the world and turning within. Meditators might seem to run away from problems instead of seeking solutions. After all, when they reopen their eyes after meditating, whatever problems they faced before remain unchanged and unresolved.

Meditation cannot fix such problems, but it can rejuvenate, energize and empower us to deal with life's challenges more effectively. Sometimes we need to temporarily withdraw and recharge our batteries, so to speak. We do this each night while sleeping. Sleep, like meditation, is not an escape; both prepare and strengthen us for the battles ahead.

Moreover, we sometimes go to bed with a problem and sleep on it, waking up in the morning with a solution. In a similar way, meditation can open our minds and allow new insights to arise. These insights can be of great help in addressing personal issues, as we will discuss in the coming chapters.

A last misconception to be considered here is the notion that meditation is narcissistic or self-centered — an unhealthy preoccupation with oneself. Meditators may appear self-obsessed when they sit alone with their eyes closed, smiling with contentment as peace and happiness fill their hearts. But if they share their peace and happiness with others, can they truly be considered self-centered?

It is a fact of life that you can only give to others what you yourself possess. To the extent you have accumulated wealth, you can share your assets with others. In the same way, to the extent love, peace, and joy have filled your heart, you can share these precious, intangible assets with others. The more peace and joy you discover in meditation, the more you have to share.

This principle has a flip side: your undesirable possessions can also be shared with others. For example, when you have a nasty cold, you might very likely give it to others. If you are in a bad mood, those close to you will certainly be affected. And if your heart is filled with hurt, sadness, and frustration, all that can be passed on to others, whether you want to or not. Meditation cannot help you avoid a cold, but it can help free you from dark moods and unpleasant emotions, allowing you to share the best of yourself with others.

Origins of Meditation

Even though this book draws upon my personal experience as a teacher and practitioner of meditation, I cannot take credit for its contents. I have been fortunate to receive a body of spiritual wisdom that has been passed down from generation to generation for millennia. This body of wisdom originated with the ancient *rishis*, the seers or sages of ancient India who lived in forest and mountain retreats more than three-thousand years ago.

Those *rishis* sought answers to life's deepest mysteries: How did the universe arise and who is its Creator? What is the purpose of life and what is our true nature? They explored vast, uncharted domains to discover truths that lay beyond the reach of ordinary human experience. The knowledge they sought could not be attained through worldly pursuits. Therefore, they turned their attention away from the world and looked within themselves instead.

The *rishis'* bold act of turning away from the world and looking within is the prototype for all forms of meditation. The *rishis* were the first to explore inner realms—regions of thought, mind, and consciousness. They were the first meditators.

In ancient times, the *rishis'* introspective pursuits must have seemed strange to common folk. Those who lived in simple agricultural societies generally focused their attention outwards—on their families and neighbors, on cooking and farming, and on the forces of nature which could grant or withhold the precious rains needed for their crops. To close one's eyes on the world and turn one's attention within was a radical, unprecedented act.

The *rishis'* fundamental shift of orientation is vividly described in the following verse from the well-known Katha Upanishad:

पराञ्चि खानि व्यतृणत्स्वयम्भूः तस्मात्पराङ् पश्यति नान्तरात्मन् ।
कश्चिद् धीराः प्रत्यगात्मानमैक्षदावृत्तचक्षुरमृतत्वमिच्छन् ॥

parānci khāni vyatrinat svayam-bhūh
tasmāt parān pashyati nāntarātman
kashcid dhīrāh pratyag-ātmānam aikshad
āvritta-cakshur amritatvam icchan

The Creator made our eyes look outwards,
therefore we see what is outside, not inside ourselves.
But some wise sages who sought immortality
turned their sight within and discovered the inner self.

KaU 4.1

In this verse, eyes represent all our senses: sight, hearing, taste, smell, and touch. They direct our attention outside, towards the world. But everything in the world is limited, finite, and ever-changing. If we seek a supreme reality that is limitless, infinite, and eternal, it will never be found so long as our attention is directed outside.

The *rishi*s deliberately defied the natural outward flow of attention. Metaphorically, they swam against the current of attention. They paddled upstream towards its origin, towards the headwaters from which consciousness itself flows. This pioneering inner journey led them to discover the knowledge they so ardently sought.

The *rishi*s expressed their inspired discoveries in Sanskrit verses which were passed down through an oral tradition for centuries before being compiled into the four Vedas, the scriptures upon which Hinduism is based. At the end of each Veda are texts known as Upanishads which include profound teachings about meditation like the verse above. In the Upanishads, the *rishi*s describe various meditation techniques and extol the lofty results attained through those practices.

The teachings of the Upanishads are also known as Vedanta, literally the last section or *anta* (end) of the Vedas. These Vedantic teachings were later incorporated into the Bhagavad Gita, the most widely studied Hindu scripture. In the sixth chapter of the Bhagavad Gita, Sri Krishna, an incarnation of God, gives detailed instructions about meditation to the mighty warrior, Arjuna. Other teachings about meditation are scattered throughout the Gita. Many important and relevant verses from the Upanishads and Bhagavad Gita are quoted in the coming pages.

In addition to the Upanishads and Bhagavad Gita, a third primary source for meditation instruction is the Yoga Sutras, a Sanskrit scripture composed by *rishi* Patanjali in the second century BCE. This scripture is a compilation of teachings about meditation that were considered ancient even at that early time.

Patanjali's text is virtually a manual for meditation. In 195 brief aphorisms known as *sutras*, he lays down a theoretical foundation for meditation and a systematic approach for its practice. Because of the text's terseness and technical complexity, it is nearly unintelligible without the aid of traditional Sanskrit commentaries. The Yoga Sutras and their commentaries are indispensable sources of guidance for meditators. In the chapters ahead, selected *sutras* will direct our exploration and provide an outline for our study.

The Upanishads, Bhagavad Gita, and Yoga Sutras have been the primary resources for generations of meditation teachers from ancient times up to our modern era. Each generation gained new insights which they passed down by writing commentaries and independent texts. In this way, a vast body of literature grew over the centuries, giving rise to a potentially bewildering assortment of systems, methods, applications, and techniques.

This immense body of Vedantic and Yogic wisdom forms the basis for this book. A thorough exploration of each and every mode of meditation is impossible, so this book concentrates on the major forms of meditation. The techniques selected have been carefully chosen to include those best suited for helping you develop your practice.

In spite of being highly selective, the range of techniques included in this book is still quite extensive. These techniques fall into four broad categories which will be explained in the following section.

Overview of Techniques

Before proceeding, let us get an overall perspective by surveying the techniques discussed in this book. From the Upanishads, Gita, Yoga Sutras, and later teachings, many distinct forms of meditation have developed. Various systems have evolved with different approaches and unique techniques. These systems differ not only in their techniques, but their objectives as well.

This is an extremely important point: different kinds of meditation have different objectives. Their goals or purposes differ in several ways. Some aim to quiet your mind or focus it on a single point. Others seek to engage your mind in a transformative process of contemplation. And still others help you detach from your mind and passively observe its activities.

Although it is an oversimplification, we could say that the various kinds of meditation are like an assortment of tools in a toolbox. Each tool has a specific purpose. A skilled handyman will choose a wrench or screwdriver of exactly the right size for the task at hand. Likewise, a skillful meditator will choose a specific technique according to the particular result desired.

The many forms of meditation can be categorized in several ways, but I find it most helpful to divide them into four broad groups as follows:

Concentration — directing your mind and focusing your attention on a particular object of meditation like your breathing, a mantra, image, or sound.

Observation — watching the activities of your mind without being involved in the process of thinking; being a detached witness to all mental activities.

Contemplation — employing specific thoughts or evoking specific emotions to produce a desired change in your patterns of thinking.

Devotion — developing a prayerful sense of being intimately connected with a chosen aspect of God; evoking feelings of reverence and adoration.

The general outline for this book is based on these four categories. Chapter One provides basic knowledge and skills. Chapters Two through Four explore forms of meditation belonging to the first category, *concentration*. The second category, *observation*, is covered in Chapter Five. Chapters Six and Seven are largely devoted to *contemplation*. *Devotion* is treated in Chapter Eight. Concluding the book, Chapters Nine and Ten explain advanced techniques and provide instructions for further practice.

As noted before, this book is not a comprehensive study of each and every form of meditation. Some techniques are left out because their overwhelming complexity would require an entire book for proper instruction. Others are omitted because they are so highly esoteric or regarded with such great reverence that they should only be learned in person from a qualified guru. The techniques included in this book have proved to be highly effective when I taught them in meditation workshops at ashrams, temples, and community centers across the country.

As a teacher of meditation, I have learned a great deal from my students over the years. When I first began teaching, I learned an especially important lesson. Back then, I assumed that the powerful techniques I had practiced for years would be equally powerful for others. But when teaching, I soon discovered that my cherished techniques were completely ineffective for a number of students.

I also discovered that some techniques which I found useless were quite powerful for others. I learned from my students that we are all unique, that every person responds differently in meditation. Therefore, there can be no single best technique. Meditation is not "one size fits all."

You must discover the techniques that are most effective for yourself. No guru can tell you, just as no one can tell you the foods you like best. To discover your favorite foods, you must sample dishes of many kinds. Likewise, to discover which forms of meditation are most effective, you must try many different techniques.

For these reasons, I avoid concentrating narrowly on one or two techniques like many teachers do. At our ashram in New Jersey, I conduct weekly guided meditation sessions in which we explore different aspects of meditation each time. Students there are encouraged to find out which techniques are most effective and practice them at home every day.

How to Use This Book

This book is a systematic introduction to the principles and practices of meditation. It begins with basic topics and simple techniques, then gradually progresses to more advanced ones. For this reason, it is important not to skip around in the book. Most chapters include a number of meditation exercises with detailed instructions for practice. It is essential to practice each of the exercises in a chapter at least once before proceeding to the next chapter.

If your goal is to learn *how* to meditate, and not merely to learn *about* meditation, then to read this book without practicing the exercises will be a waste of time. You cannot learn to cook by reading a cookbook; you must go to the kitchen and try out the recipes for yourself. Likewise, you cannot learn to meditate just by reading this book. You must sit down, close your eyes, and practice each technique, one at a time, following the instructions provided.

This book includes a total of 35 meditation exercises. If you meditate once a day and practice one exercise each time, it will take more than a month to finish this book. But you might find it quite helpful to practice each exercise several times before proceeding. Then many months can be spent going through this book. But there is no need to hurry. In fact, the longer you take to finish this book and the more time you spend practicing the meditation exercises, the greater will be your benefit.

After finishing this book, you can choose the techniques you found most effective and use them for further practice. The last chapter is devoted to helping you build an ongoing practice that will reward you day by day with inner peace and spiritual growth. Let us begin this journey of exploration with the first chapter, Building a Strong Foundation for Personal Practice.

CHAPTER ONE

BUILDING A STRONG FOUNDATION FOR PERSONAL PRACTICE

Meditation is a learned skill. No one is born with a natural aptitude for meditation, nor can special rituals confer the ability to meditate. Meditation truly is a learned skill. And it is learned the same way you learn other skills. How did you learn to drive a car? How did you learn to cook, use a computer, or play a musical instrument?

To learn a skill, two basic factors are necessary — instruction and practice. With the right training and sufficient practice, you could probably learn to fly an airplane or perform surgery. Fortunately, most meditation techniques are not as difficult as flying or surgery. In fact, they are quite simple.

So, how difficult can it be to meditate? Actually, without adequate instruction and practice, even simple techniques are impossibly difficult. A novice tennis player will lose every game if he fails to take lessons and plays rarely. Learning to meditate is no different. It is simply a matter of getting proper instruction and keeping up your practice. There are no secrets or shortcuts.

When learning any new skill, it is essential to master the basics before moving on to more advanced aspects. This is certainly true of meditation. Unless the fundamentals are mastered, there is no possibility of success with advanced techniques. The basics are like the foundation for a tall building; its strength depends entirely on the strength of its foundation.

A beautiful analogy compares the beginning practice of meditation to a young sapling. A sapling can grow only as tall as its roots are deep. If its roots are shallow due to rocky soil, its growth will be stunted. Shallow roots will also leave it vulnerable to being blown down in a storm. In the same way, insufficient practice of basic techniques can stunt your progress in meditation. And if your practice is weak, you might abandon it altogether when the storms of life pull your attention away.

On the other hand, the deeper a sapling's roots have spread, the taller it can grow and the better it can resist violent winds. Similarly, the stronger your practice has grown, the further you can progress with advanced techniques and the better you can maintain your practice while dealing with the challenges of life.

This chapter will help you establish a strong foundation on which you can build a deeply rewarding practice of meditation. Exercises presented later in this chapter will guide you step by step to master some of the basic skills you will need for more advanced techniques taught in later chapters.

Yoga's Eight-Step System of Meditation

There is no better theoretical foundation for the practice of meditation than Pantanjali's Yoga Sutras. The word yoga comes from the Sanskrit verbal root, *yuj*, to which our English word yoke is also related. Based on this root, yoga has two key meanings—to *unite* and to *control*.

A yoke is used to harness an animal to pull a plow or cart. The strong, wooden yoke serves both to *control* the animal's movements and also to join or *unite* it to the cart. These two functions are essential for meditation in which powerful techniques are used to bring your mind under *control* and eventually *unite* it with an object of meditation.

Patanjali provides a systematic method for controlling the mind and leading it to a state of union. His method consists of a series of eight steps which he calls *anga*s or limbs. These eight limbs are like the rungs in a ladder; each allows you to advance to the next step. Patanjali identifies all eight *anga*s in the following *sutra*:

यमनियमासनप्राणायामप्रत्याहारधारणाध्यानसमाधयोऽष्टावङ्गानि ॥

yama-niyamāsana-prāṇāyāma-pratyāhāra-
dhāraṇā-dhyāna-samādhayo 'shtāvangāni

The eight limbs of yoga are *yama, niyama, āsana, prāṇāyāma, pratyāhāra, dhāranā, dhyāna* and *samādhi*.

YS 2.29

The meaning of each *anga* can be briefly explained as follows:

Yama — restraint; avoidance of immoral acts

Niyama — injunction; performance of moral disciplines

Āsana — seated posture; sitting correctly for meditation

Prāṇāyāma — breath control; breathing exercises

Pratyāhāra — sense withdrawal; turning attention within

Dhāranā — concentration; narrowly focusing attention

Dhyāna — meditation; uninterrupted flow of attention

Samādhi — complete absorption in object of meditation

The systematic arrangement of these steps can easily be seen. *Yama* and *niyama* prepare you for practice which begins by sitting with proper posture: *āsana*. Then you perform breathing exercises to settle your mind: *prāṇāyāma*. Next, you withdraw your attention from the world around you: *pratyāhāra*. Then you concentrate your attention on an object of meditation: *dhāranā*. Eventually, your attention flows towards the object of meditation without interruption: *dhyāna*.

Each of these steps successively helps bring your mind under control. They lead to the eighth and last limb of yoga, *samādhi* which is a state of union. Thus both meanings of yoga — to unite and to control — are present in the eight *angas*.

This brief description of yoga's limbs is intended only to show the orderly progression from one *anga* to the next. Complete explanations of all eight are spread over several chapters in this book, following their given order. The first three — *yama, niyama*, and *āsana* — are discussed in this chapter.

Yama and *Niyama*, Prohibitions and Injunctions

Yama and *niyama* may be considered together since they are closely related. As mentioned before, *yama* means restraint or prohibition. This *anga* prohibits meditators from certain unethical acts like lying and stealing. *Niyama* means observance or injunction. It enjoins meditators to perform particular moral disciplines like prayer and scriptural study.

At first, it might seem strange that an eight-step system of meditation would include moral prohibitions and injunctions as the first two steps. What do such principles have to do with meditation? If meditation were like other skills, these two *anga*s would be superfluous, totally unnecessary. But meditation is quite unlike cooking or playing tennis and therefore has some unique requirements. Let us see why *yama* and *niyama* are essential for meditation.

If a tennis player is involved in a big argument just before playing a match, the argument would probably be forgotten as he concentrated on the game. But if a meditator has a nasty argument just before sitting to practice, the effects of that argument would be striking. During meditation, the meditator's thoughts would be drawn to the argument again and again, completely ruining his practice.

Unlike tennis, meditation is a subtle, introspective activity. It does not require physical strength or manual dexterity, but it does require an attentive, undistracted mind. Just as you cannot play tennis with a broken arm, you cannot meditate when your mind is distracted or preoccupied. Such distractions are inevitable whenever you are entangled in strife or conflict, as was the meditator in this example.

According to the Vedic *rishis*, the basic cause for strife and conflict is behaving contrary to the moral and ethical principles of dharma, the principles that define righteous life. Lying, cheating, injuring, and similar deeds create discord in life. My guru is fond of saying that when you oppose or "rub up" against dharma, it is like rubbing your bare arm against the rough bark of a tree. "Who rubs whom?" he asks. The tree remains unharmed, but your arm would be scratched and bleeding. In the same way, those who transgress dharma are themselves harmed in the process by being plunged into discord and turmoil.

Living a life of dharma helps you remain free from such discord so your mind can be undistracted and fully available for meditation. That is why the first two limbs of yoga, *yama* and *niyama*, address righteous and unrighteous behaviors. Patanjali defines these two *angas* in the following *sutras*:

अहिंसासत्यास्तेयब्रह्मचर्यापरिग्रहा यमाः ॥
शौचसन्तोषतपःस्वाध्यायेश्वरप्रणिधानानि नियमाः ॥

ahimsā-satyāsteya-brahmacaryāparigrahā yamaḥ
shauca-santosha-tapah-svādhyāyeshvara-pranidhānāni niyamāḥ

YS 2.30, 32

The five *yamas* or prohibitions are:

ahimsā – refraining from causing harm to others

satya – speaking truthfully, refraining from falsehoods

asteya – refraining from stealing

brahmacarya – refraining from improper sexual activity

aparigraha – refraining from grasping or possessiveness

The five *niyamas* or injunctions are:

shauca – maintaining cleanliness of mind and body

santosha – maintaining contentment and composure

tapas – practice of austerities like fasting

svādhyāya – undertaking regular scriptural study

īshvara pranidhāna – being devoted to God

The five *yamas* and five *niyamas* guide us to follow the path of righteousness and live a life of dharma. Sometimes they are humorously referred to as the ten commandments of yoga. But they are utterly unlike the biblical mandates given to Moses. Those commandments were to be followed to avoid God's wrath and eternal damnation. In contrast, the *yamas* and *niyamas* have an entirely different purpose. They instruct us to follow dharma for the sake of a conflict-free life that will support our practice of meditation.

Sitting for Meditation

Now we come to the third of the eight limbs: *āsana* or posture. Today, the word *āsana* brings to mind the convoluted twisting postures used by practitioners of *hatha* yoga. You might be familiar with the *padmāsana* or lotus pose in which you sit with your left foot resting on your right thigh and your right foot resting on your left thigh. But what do such postures have to do with meditation? If you are not particularly limber and sit in *padmāsana* to meditate, you would probably find it quite uncomfortable. Before long, your limbs would ache so badly that you could meditate only on the intense pain in your legs!

This observation demonstrates an important fact — the actual relationship between *āsana* and meditation is not well understood. For example, in many yoga studios across the country, *āsana*s alone are practiced. Since *āsana*s are just one of yoga's eight limbs, students in those studios are missing out on the remaining seven. Further, *āsana* is one of the preparatory limbs of yoga; it is meant to prepare you for meditation. One who practices *āsana*s but fails to meditate is like a cook who prepares a meal and leaves it in the kitchen, uneaten.

To correctly understand the role of *āsana* in meditation, we turn again to Patanjali's *sutra*s where he defines *āsana* as follows:

स्थिरसुखमासनम् ॥
sthira-sukham āsanam

One's seated posture must be stable and comfortable.

YS 2.46

The word *āsana* is derived from a verbal root that means to sit. Here, Patanjali describes the seated posture to be used for meditation. He simply says it must be *sthira* and *sukha*, stable and comfortable. Your body must be well-supported and pain-free for meditation. Then what about the convoluted postures practiced in yoga studios? Patanjali says nothing about them. The only posture described in the Yoga Sutras is the one above.

Hatha yoga's elaborate system of *āsana*s as practiced to-day evolved over many centuries. The original purpose of those *āsana*s was to prepare your body for extended periods of seated meditation. Advanced meditators must be able to sit for hours without being distracted by pain or the need to shift their limbs. Could you sit perfectly motionless for several hours and remain comfortable, even in a well-stuffed chair? If you practiced the complex *āsanas* of *hatha* yoga regularly, you most likely could. And that indeed is the purpose of those postures—to prepare your body for the demands of extended meditation sessions.

If you do not plan to meditate for hours at a time, you probably don't need to perform those *āsanas*. But it is certainly necessary to sit with proper posture for meditation, remaining stable and comfortable. If you sit on the floor, a cushion beneath you and support for your back may be necessary. If you find sitting in a chair more comfortable, that is a perfectly acceptable option.

Some very practical advice about posture is found in the sixth chapter of the Bhagavad Gita:

समं कायशिरोग्रीवं धारयन्नचलं स्थिरः ।
संप्रेक्ष्य नासिकाग्रं स्वं दिशश्चानवलोकयन् ॥

*samam kāya-shiro-grīvam dhārayann acalam sthirah
samprekshya nāsikāgram svam dishash cānavalokayan*

Remain firm and still, holding your body, head, and neck erect, gazing at the tip of your nose without looking elsewhere.

BG 6.13

This verse stresses the importance of keeping your back straight. Slumping forward can cause back pain. Leaning backwards can make you drowsy.

"Gazing at the tip of your nose" is an ancient saying that means to cast your gaze downwards, past your nose and towards the ground in front of you, through eyelids that are barely closed. Your eyes should be closed very gently to avoid creating any tension in the muscles of your face. You can even allow a little sliver of light to enter through your eyelashes.

Your hands may be placed comfortably in your lap or on your knees. There is no single correct manner to place your hands, although some Buddhist traditions specify that the right hand should cradle the left with the tips of both thumbs touching each other. You might find it helpful to experiment with different positions and find out what feels most comfortable for you. Then you should settle on one position and use it consistently.

Further, it is of the utmost importance to choose an appropriate place for meditation. Places affect the way we feel. You feel very different at work, at home, or at a sacred place like a temple or ashram. Your choice of location can either enhance your meditation or impair it. For example, if you sit on your bed to meditate, you are likely to feel sleepy. If you sit on a chair near a television, you might be more subject to distractions.

It is desirable to set aside a place in your home exclusively dedicated to meditation, prayer, and spiritual study. If you already have an altar or prayer room in your home, that might be the best place. Otherwise, you can create a small space in a quiet corner. You can furnish it with a cushion or suitable chair, and decorate it with sacred objects. The effort you make in creating a special, sacred space for meditation can significantly strengthen your practice.

It is best to meditate in the same place every time. In this way, a beneficial mental association with that location will develop. After many meditation sessions, your mind will spontaneously quiet down as soon as you sit there. Over time, your sacred place will become a cherished spot to which you eagerly return again and again for practice.

Preparing to Meditate

Many activities require some preparation. Each night before going to bed, you brush your teeth, adjust your bedding, and turn off the light. This routine prepares you to get a good night's sleep. Likewise, there are certain steps to be followed before meditation. These steps form a standard routine that you can use to begin each session. The basic steps of preparation are:

1) *Āsana* – seated posture, sitting comfortably with proper posture in a quiet, suitable place.

2) *Sankalpa* – affirmation, giving yourself permission to turn your attention away from worldly activities.

3) Relaxation – releasing any tension found in each part of your body.

Āsana has already been discussed, so we can turn to the second step, *sankalpa*. Throughout each day, you are busy solving problems, coping with difficulties, and sometimes dealing with crises. When you sit and close your eyes for meditation, all those activities remain present in your mind. When you try to turn your attention away from them, your mind will often resist.

The important issues in your life certainly deserve attention; it would be irresponsible to ignore them. But as discussed in the introduction, meditation is not ignoring or running away from problems. Yet many of us feel so highly responsible that we find it difficult to let go of worldly concerns at the time of meditation. We have appointments to keep, groceries to buy, and phone calls to return. If we feel reluctant to let go of those matters during meditation, we will bring them to mind again and again like a cow chewing its cud.

A powerful means for temporarily setting aside your concerns is a *sankalpa*, an affirmation of your commitment or intention to meditate. The *sankalpa* for meditation has two parts. First, you acknowledge the many pressing concerns and unresolved issues in your life. Second, you give yourself permission to set them all aside, just for the duration of meditation.

The *sankalpa* can be in the form of a dialogue with your own mind, such as:

> "Hello, mind. It is time to meditate now. I know you have many concerns and unresolved issues, but this is not the right time to think about them. Please set them aside while we meditate, just for the next half-hour or so. After meditating, you will feel refreshed and ready to address all those matters."

Another version of this *sankalpa* can be found in Exercise 1-1 later in this chapter.

Such a *sankalpa* helps bring about a crucial transition necessary at the very start of meditation when your attention must be completely redirected. It must be withdrawn from the world outside and turned towards your mind itself. A *sankalpa* helps redirect your attention in this way. It also helps prevent worries and concerns from arising as you meditate. These can push their way into your mind at any time during your practice. Starting with a *sankalpa* helps minimize such distractions.

The third and final step of preparation is to release any tension from the muscles of your body. Often, tension is unconsciously held in certain muscles. Such tension can lead to discomfort when you try to sit motionless for more than a few minutes. If your body is thoroughly relaxed, you will find it much easier to sit still for twenty to thirty minutes or longer.

A simple progressive relaxation exercise can be used to get ready for meditation. In this exercise, you direct your attention to each part of your body, one part at a time. At each point, you first observe any tension being held there, then you allow it to be released. Details of this procedure are provided in Exercise 1-1.

There is a second but equally important purpose for this progressive relaxation exercise. Concentrating on your body is actually the first step in turning your attention from outside to inside. When preparing to meditate, you can redirect your attention in three steps or stages. First, you direct your attention towards your body using the progressive relaxation exercise. Then, you turn it towards your breath using techniques to be explained later in this chapter. Finally, you direct your attention towards your mind. This gradual, step by step approach is especially helpful for beginning meditators.

Throughout this book, meditation exercises are provided that describe specific techniques you can learn, practice, and later incorporate into your own meditation routine. The basic steps of preparation to be performed at the beginning of each meditation session are given in the following exercise.

Exercise 1-1

Basic Steps of Preparation

Āsana:

In a suitable, quiet place, sit on a cushion or chair with your back erect, your shoulders relaxed, and your chin tilted down very slightly. Place your hands comfortably in your lap or on your knees. Close your eyes very gently and take several deep breaths to get settled down.

Sankalpa:

Affirm your intention and commitment as follows: "I have a busy, complicated life filled with duties, responsibilities, and unresolved issues. I do not want to be distracted by all that during meditation. So right now, I give myself permission to set all that aside, just for the duration of this meditation. I can afford to give myself fully and exclusively to this meditation, knowing that when it is over, I can return to my worldly concerns and handle them even more effectively as a result of meditating."

Progressive Relaxation:

Turn your attention to each part of your body listed below, one at a time. Become aware of sensations like the feeling of pressure, warmth or coolness, or the touch of your clothing. Take note of any tension being held in the muscles there. Then allow those muscles to relax completely, letting go of any tension before moving on to the next part. Take at least 10-15 seconds for each part.

1. Feet, ankles, and calves
2. Knees and thighs
3. Trunk
4. Lower back and stomach
5. Upper back and chest
6. Shoulders
7. Arms
8. Hands
9. Neck, jaw, and mouth
10. Eyes and forehead

The preceding exercise should be performed at the beginning of each meditation session. After you learn it well, feel free to change or adapt it in any way that makes it more effective for your personal practice.

Being in the Present Moment

One of the first things you are likely to discover when you start to meditate is that your mind is subject to countless distractions. Unseen inner forces, including the personal concerns and unresolved issues discussed before, seem eager to wrench your mind away and drag it in one direction or another.

Most often, your mind is dragged along one of two routes—back to the past or forward into the future. A distracted mind is rarely found in the present moment. It can usually be found wandering amongst memories of past events or worrying about difficulties waiting in the future. Memories and worries seem to linger within, ready to hijack your attention, as though plotting to kidnap your mind.

Painful memories can forcibly drag your mind back to the past. If a friend said something particularly hurtful to you yesterday, today's meditation session can be affected. Worry, on the other hand, can drag your thoughts into the future. If you are waiting for the results of a recent biopsy, your mind can easily get caught up in pondering future scenarios.

Painful memories and nagging worries are a normal part of life; they cannot be avoided. Yet their power to drag your mind into the past or future during meditation must be resisted. The solution is to fix your attention on the present moment, on what is happening right now. In the present moment, there is no past or future, no memories or worries. There is only the experience of *now*.

To keep your mind fixed on the present, it is helpful to observe something that fluctuates from moment to moment, changing constantly. And for meditation, it should be something inside you, not outside. For these reasons, the practice of observing your breath is a powerful and widely used meditation technique

At rest, you breathe about twelve times a minute. In just five seconds, you complete a full cycle of filling your lungs with air and expelling it. This natural rhythm of inhalation and exhalation is an ideal focal point for meditation. By directing your attention towards this continual rhythm, your mind can be restrained from wandering into the past or future. With this technique, you can eventually train your mind to remain fixed in the present moment during meditation.

Observing Your Breath—*Prāna Vikshana*

In many forms of meditation, your attention must be concentrated upon a suitable object like a mantra, sound, or image. Your breath, too, can become an object of meditation. One technique of meditating on your breath is called *prāna vikshana*, observing (*vikshana*) your breath (*prāna*).

The primary meaning of *prāna* is life-force. The air you breathe is essential for life. In *prāna vikshana*, you observe the rhythmic flow of life-giving air as it enters your body with each inhalation and is expelled with each exhalation. This technique differs from *prānāyāma*, the breathing exercises which constitute the fourth limb of yoga (discussed in the next chapter). In *prāna vīkshana*, there is no attempt to control or regulate your breathing as in *prānāyāma* techniques; it is simply a matter of observing your breath.

The following meditation exercise provides instructions for the practice of *prāna vīkshana*.

Exercise 1-2

Observing Your Breath – *Prāna Vīkshana*

Preparation:

Following the steps in Exercise 1-1, sit with proper posture, close your eyes, make a *sankalpa* to set aside your concerns, and perform the progressive relaxation exercise.

Practice:

Breathe only through your nose and turn your attention to your breath. Observe the process of inhalation and exhalation by tracing the passage of air with each breath. As you inhale, observe the air entering your nostrils, traveling down your windpipe, and filling your lungs. As you exhale, observe the air being released from your lungs, traveling up your windpipe, and leaving your nostrils. Breathe at a normal rate.

To help prevent your mind from wandering, a useful technique is to count mentally as you observe your breath. With each inhalation, count 1....2....3.... as you trace the passage of air. With each exhalation, count 4....5....6.... as you again trace the passage of air. Do not change the speed of your breathing; match the counting to your natural rhythm. Continue for ten minutes or more.

Conclusion:

Stop counting after completing an exhalation. Take a few moments to observe how your body and mind feel before slowly opening your eyes.

Prāna vīkshana is a valuable technique for all meditators. For beginners, it is a simple and effective means for training your mind to remain in the present moment. For advanced practitioners, *prāna vīkshana* is often used in conjunction with other techniques, as will be discussed in coming chapters.

Establishing a Regular Practice

Certain activities, like bathing and brushing your teeth, need to be performed every day. Bathing just once a week is not enough. Likewise, weekly meditation is not enough. To find inner peace and nurture your process of spiritual growth, daily practice is indispensable. Here are some guidelines for establishing a regular, daily practice.

First, practice at a time of day that suits you. If your schedule does not permit you to meditate in the morning, then find a suitable time later in the day. But once you have found a time that works well for you, stay with it. Every day at that same time, sit at your chosen place and meditate. Before long, this will become a pleasant habit like your daily shower.

Some believe that the best time for meditation is *brahma muhurtam*, the interval between four and five in the morning. That may have been true long ago, before the advent of electric lighting. Back then, everyone went to bed by nine o'clock. But today, such a schedule would be highly impractical for most meditators.

To meditate shortly after waking up or just before going to sleep may pose difficulties for some. Meditation requires a mind that is bright and alert. If you are quite drowsy just after rising or before bedtime, it might be best to choose other times to meditate. If possible, find the time of day when your mind is at its brightest and arrange your schedule so that you can meditate then. The basic principle here is to find the time that works best for you.

How long should you meditate each day? When I first began, I returned from a meditation workshop feeling so enthusiastic that I resolved to meditate for 45 minutes each day. The following morning, I eagerly sat to practice the technique I learned at the workshop. After a while, I peeked at a clock to check the time because I did not want to be late for work. Only 30 minutes had elapsed, so I closed my eyes and continued. When I checked again later, 35 minutes had passed. And the next time I checked, I found that exactly 36 minutes had elapsed!

I became restless and uncomfortable towards the end of that first session, but I forced myself to complete the full 45 minutes. The next morning, I sat to meditate with much less enthusiasm, and I struggled even more to complete the allotted time. On the third morning, I turned off my alarm clock and went back to sleep for 45 minutes. My daily practice had quickly come to an end.

I made two mistakes. One was to overestimate my ability to sit comfortably for a prolonged time. The other was to force myself to finish the long sessions. By doing so, I made my practice unpleasant and that soon discouraged me from continuing. I was like a person with a new exercise routine who overexerts himself on the first day and then aches so badly that he immediately gives up the routine.

If your meditation routine is unpleasant, it can be extremely difficult to maintain your practice, especially if you have little free time. You can almost always find time for things you enjoy. Even with a busy schedule, you can find time to eat, chat with friends, or watch a favorite television show. But when time is short, unpleasant activities are the first to be set aside. If you do not enjoy your practice, meditation is likely to fall to the bottom of your to-do list.

For these reasons, it is essential to keep your practice pleasant. You can avoid making it tedious by keeping it short in length. Ten minutes is a good length to start with. Ten minutes is long enough to reap some benefit but short enough to prevent you from using everyone's favorite excuse, "I don't have enough time."

Meditating for just ten minutes a day is like planting a seed. A tiny seed can grow into a tall tree. In the same way, ten minutes of daily meditation can put down roots and grow into a wonderful practice. Before long, you can develop a love for meditation and look forward to your appointed time each day. After a while, you might find yourself meditating for twenty or thirty minutes or more, not because you think you *should* meditate longer, but because you *want* to.

CHAPTER TWO

TURNING WITHIN: FINDING INNER PEACE

We all seek happiness. We want joy, peace, and contentment in life. We pursue these in our families, with our friends, through work and play, and in the simple comforts of life. Ironically, most of us would readily admit that the true source of happiness is inside us. We intuitively know that contentment and peace come from within. In spite of this, we ordinarily look for happiness outside in the world, overlooking the possibility of finding it within.

As discussed in the introduction, the ancient *rishi*s turned their attention away from the world and searched within themselves. They discovered the source of happiness and peace to be one's true self, *ātmā*. That source is referred to in various ways—inner divinity, God's sacred presence within, *sat cit ānanda*, etc.

About that inner source, the Katha Upanishad says:

47

तमात्मस्थं येऽनुपश्यन्ति धीरास्तेषां शान्तिः शाश्वती नेतरेषाम् ।

tam ātmastham ye 'nupashyanti dhīrās
teshām shāntih shāshvatī netareshām

The wise ones who discover *that* within themselves
gain eternal peace, but not others.

KaU 2.2.13

What exactly is *that*? A commentary on this Upanishad by the renowned eighth-century teacher of Vedanta, Shankara, describes it as "the one, all-pervasive, all-powerful Supreme Being." *That* is what abides within us all.

Now we come to a crucial question: If our true nature is divine, if God dwells within us as the source of eternal peace, *shānti*, then why is peace so often absent from our lives? Why don't we always feel peaceful?

The teachings of Vedanta show that all experiences, including the experience of peace, take place in our minds. Therefore, our minds must be available and open for the experience of peace. But when our minds are filled with frustration, sadness, or anger, there is no room for peace to enter. Even though the source of *shānti* is always present, its experience can be obstructed by our thoughts and emotions. In other words, the peace in our hearts gets overpowered by the commotion in our minds.

To understand this better, imagine being in a crowded railway station, filled with the clamor of shouting voices, roaring engines, and clattering cars. If someone speaks to you from ten feet away, you might see his mouth moving and yet not hear a word he says. Even though the sound of his voice physically reaches your ears, it cannot be heard because it is overwhelmed by the noise. In the same way, even though God dwells in your heart as the source of *shānti*, peace cannot be experienced if it is overwhelmed by the noisy clamor in your mind. Frustration, sadness, anger, and the like can become so strident that all other experiences are drowned out.

The fact that mental clamor can obstruct your experience of peace is indicated by the very meaning of the word *shānti*. It comes from the verbal root *sham* which means to be quiet or silent. When mental activities subside and your mind becomes relatively quiet, you feel peaceful. Your mind need not be totally silent to experience peace, just as the railway station need not be totally silent to hear someone. The quieter your mind becomes, the more peaceful you feel.

This observation leads to a remarkable conclusion—*shānti* is not produced by mental activities; it is experienced in their absence. Mental activities are called *vrittis* which literally means the movements of your mind. *Vrittis* are like waves moving across the surface of a pond. When waves disturb a pond's surface, you cannot see the fish below. Likewise, when your mind is agitated by *vrittis*, the peace within cannot be experienced. But the fish can be easily seen when only a few tiny ripples remain on the pond. So too, peace is effortlessly experienced when only a few *vrittis* remain in your mind.

Meditation helps calm the waves of your mind. Using certain techniques, your mind can be made profoundly silent and you can experience immense peace arising from the divine source within. The Bhagavad Gita explains this nicely:

यत्रोपरमते चित्तं निरुद्धं योगसेवया ।
यत्र चैवात्मनात्मानं पश्यन्नात्मनि तुष्यति ॥

yatroparamate cittam niruddham yogasevayā
yatra caivātmanātmānam pashyann ātmani tushyati

When the mind is silenced by meditation, one discovers
the true self, *ātmā*, and finds contentment in oneself.

BG 6.20

When your mind has been quieted by meditation, peace arises spontaneously from the source within, from your true nature. No further effort is required.

Quieting Your Mind

Not surprisingly, these same principles are taught in the Yoga Sutras. The need to quiet your mind to find inner peace is declared at its very beginning. Immediately after the opening *sutra*, Patanjali says with amazing clarity and brevity:

योगश्चित्तवृत्तिनिरोधः ॥ तदा द्रष्टुः स्वरूपेऽवस्थानम् ॥
yogash citta-vritti-nirodhah | tadā drashtuh svarūpe 'vasthānam

> Yoga is the cessation of all mental activities.
> Then, the meditator abides in one's true nature.
>
> YS 1.2-3

Yoga, in this context, means the practice of meditation. The particular practice described here is the cessation or restraint (*nirodhah*) of all movements (*vritti*) of the mind (*citta*). When the mind is completely silenced, one abides in the true self, *ātmā*, the inner divinity, the source of *shānti*. Much of Patanjali's text is devoted to explaining how the mind can be silenced.

To make your mind absolutely silent can be extraordinarily difficult. In meditation, you cannot simply turn off your thoughts. Commanding your mind to stop is futile because it seems to have its own agenda — you want to meditate but it wants to wander. As hard as you try to silence your thoughts, your mind can easily resist and continue to wander.

A common metaphor compares minds to the restless, mischievous monkeys seen throughout India. Monkeys jump from tree to tree as rapidly as your mind can jump from one thought to another. Monkeys are also quite clever. Groups of them sometimes congregate near temples and pounce upon unsuspecting worshipers bringing food to be offered. I have a funny anecdote about a monkey that suggests how restless minds can be brought under control.

Once, I visited an ashram in South India with a friend who was a *brahmachari*, a novice monk. Each morning, he washed his white robes by hand and hung them on a clothesline outside to dry. The ashram was surrounded by a jungle teeming with monkeys. One day, a particularly mis-chievous monkey pulled his clothes off the line and rolled around on the ground with them in play.

My friend faced a dilemma about how to retrieve his robes. He could grab a stick and chase after the playful creature, but it would surely outrun him. Instead, he went to his room and returned with a banana. The monkey ran for the banana, abandoning the clothes which my friend quickly retrieved.

This story aptly illustrates the challenge of controlling your mind. Just as the monkey could outrun my friend's assault with a stick, your mind can elude your forceful, direct attempts to silence it. But just as the monkey could not resist a tasty fruit, in the same way, your mind will yield to approaches that are gentle, pleasing, and soothing. The banana and stick represent two opposite approaches to controlling your mind. These same contrasting options are seen in the old saying about using a carrot or a stick to encourage someone, a saying based on the use of carrots and sticks long ago to motivate ornery donkeys.

Since most of us have little contact with monkeys or donkeys, it might be helpful to draw upon a more common experience — caring for a crying baby. If you try to quiet an infant by shouting, "Shut up!" she will only cry more loudly. Harsh, forceful attempts are doomed to failure. But if you respond by giving her a cuddly toy or juice to drink, she is much more likely to stop crying.

Applying these insights to the challenge of quieting your mind, it is clear that forceful efforts to drive your mind into a state of silence are destined to fail. On the other hand, techniques that are pleasant and comforting are much more likely to work. Most meditation techniques employ this latter principle. Gentle methods like the calming repetition of a mantra or breathing exercises that soothe your nerves can be remarkably effective in quieting your mind.

Prāṇāyāma — Breathing Exercises

The breathing exercises collectively known as *prāṇāyāma* are ideal for gently calming your mind and gradually making it quiet. That is why Patanjali establishes *prāṇāyāma* as the fourth of yoga's eight limbs, following *yama, niyama,* and *āsana* discussed in the last chapter. He introduces *prāṇāyāma* in the following *sutra*:

प्रच्छर्दनविधारणाभ्यां वा प्राणस्य ॥

pracchardana-vidhāranābhyām vā pranasya

(The mind is calmed) by retention and exhalation of the breath.

YS 1.34

Regulation of breathing has a powerful effect on the nervous system, as well understood by medical science. Slow, deep breathing directly affects the *autonomic nervous system* which controls heart rate, blood pressure, digestion, etc. This system has two branches. One is the *sympathetic nervous system* which increases heart rate and blood pressure in response to perceived threats. It produces the well-known "fight or flight" response. The other branch is the *parasympathetic nervous system* which has the opposite effect. It lowers your heart rate and blood pressure while increasing digestion and excretion.

Most forms of *pranāyāma* stimulate the parasympathetic nervous system. They calm your body by triggering what is called the "rest and digest" response. And as your body becomes more relaxed, your mind responds by becoming more quiet. It does so due to a fundamental connection between body and mind.

Your body and mind are intimately connected; what happens to one affects the other. When your heart rate and blood pressure are reduced by *pranāyāma*, your mind becomes more calm. Conversely, if you use a meditation technique to calm your mind, your heart rate and blood pressure will decrease.

The importance of this body-mind connection is being increasingly recognized by medical science. Doctors now understand that the state of their patients' minds affects the process of healing. Today, simple forms of meditation and *pranāyāma* are taught as relaxation techniques to patients in medical clinics across the country. It is interesting to note that the body-mind connection was well understood by ancient yogis long before the advent of modern medicine.

Patanjali defines the basic practice of *prāṇāyāma* as follows:

तस्मिन्सति श्वासप्रश्वासयोर्गतिविच्छेदः प्राणायामः ॥

tasmin sati shvāsa-prashvāsayor gati-vicchedah prāṇāyāmah

Then (following the prior limb, *āsana*),
prāṇāyāma is regulating the flow of inhalation and exhalation.

YS 2.49

Regulating your inhalation and exhalation by making them slow and deep triggers your parasympathetic nervous system and the "rest and digest" response. Due to the body-mind connection, this helps quiet your mind.

Nādi Shodhana — Cleansing the Nerves

There are many kinds of *prāṇāyāma*, but the technique known as *nādi shodhana* is especially intended to calm your nervous system. Every day, you encounter many stressful events — careless drivers, angry bosses, stacks of unpaid bills, etc. Each of these events can trigger your "fight or flight" response. When this happens repeatedly, stress gradually builds up in your body and mind. *Nādi shodhana* helps release this accumulated stress.

Nādi shodhana means cleansing (*shodhana*) the nerves (*nādi*). It is also known as *anuloma viloma* which is loosely translated as alternate nostril breathing. In this practice, your breath is alternately directed through your left and right nostrils by closing one nostril at a time with the fingers of your right hand.

There are two methods of closing the nostrils, as described in the following illustrations.

Hand Position for *Nādi Shodhana*

With your right hand, bend your index and middle fingers down, folding them into your palm, leaving your thumb and remaining fingers free. Bring your hand in front of your face with your thumb and ring finger next to either side of your nose. If helpful, you can support your right arm by bracing its elbow with your left hand.

the right side of your nose ......
eft nostril, shift your hand
s your ring finger gently
Use as little pressure as

Press your thumb gently a
to close the right nostril. To clos
to release the right nostril an
against the left side of your n
possible to stop the flow of air.

Alternate Hand Position for *Nādi Shodhana*

Extend the index and middle fingers of your right hand and place them on your forehead, between your eyebrows. Bend your thumb and ring fingers down, next to either side of your nose. If helpful, you can support your right arm by bracing its elbow with your left hand.

Press your thumb gently against the right side of your nose to close the right nostril. To close the left nostril, shift your hand to release the right nostril and press your ring finger gently against the left side of your nose. Use as little pressure as possible to stop the flow of air.

Try both of the above methods and choose whichever seems more comfortable for you.

The following exercise will teach you the various steps necessary for *nādi shodhana*. Be sure to adjust your breathing so that you remain comfortable at all times. You should never feel lightheaded or short of breath while performing any *prānāyāma* technique.

Exercise 2-1

Learning *Nādi Shodhana*

Perform each of the five steps below. After each step, rest your hands in your lap for a few moments before continuing.

1) Using either of the hand positions previously described, gently close your right nostril. Inhale and exhale through your left nostril for five to ten breaths.

2) Gently close your left nostril. Inhale and exhale through your right nostril for five to ten breaths.

3) Close your right nostril and inhale through the left. Then shift your hand to close your left nostril and exhale through the right. Repeat this sequence five to ten times.

4) Close your left nostril and inhale through the right. Then shift your hand to close your right nostril and exhale through the left. Repeat this sequence five to ten times.

5) Close your right nostril and inhale through the left. Then shift your hand to close your left nostril and exhale through the right. Next, without moving your hand, inhale through your right nostril. Then shift your hand to close your right nostril and exhale through the left. Repeat this sequence five to ten times.

The above exercise is not intended for regular practice. This step by step approach is meant to familiarize you with the details of *nādi shodhana*. For regular practice, you should follow the procedure in Step 5 which is a two breath sequence: 1) inhale left and exhale right, 2) inhale right and exhale left. The proper use of this technique for meditation is described in the following meditation exercise.

Exercise 2-2

Nādi Shodhana

Preparation:

Following the steps in Exercise 1-1, sit with proper posture, close your eyes, make a *sankalpa* to set aside your concerns, and perform the progressive relaxation exercise.

Practice:

Using either of the hand positions previously described, close your right nostril and inhale through the left. Then shift your hand to close your left nostril and exhale through the right. Next, without moving your hand, inhale through your right nostril. Then shift your hand to close your right nostril and exhale through the left. Repeat this entire sequence.

Continue for ten minutes or more, adjusting your breathing so that you remain completely comfortable at all times.

Options:

After you have mastered the basics of this technique, you can deepen your practice by 1) inhaling a bit more deeply, 2) pausing briefly between inhalation and exhalation, 3) pausing briefly between exhalation and inhalation. It is important to keep each pause brief enough so that you never feel short of breath.

Conclusion:

Rest your hands in your lap and allow your breathing to return to normal. Observe how you feel for a few moments before slowly opening your eyes.

Relationship between Breath and Mind

An important aspect of the previously discussed body-mind connection is the close relationship between your breathing and your state of mind. This relationship can easily be observed. When you feel stressed, anxious, or angry, your breathing tends to become rapid and shallow. But when you sit at home in your favorite chair to relax, your breathing slows and becomes deeper.

This connection works both ways. Not only does your state of mind affect your breathing, but the nature of your breathing affects your mind. The effect of breathing on your mind is much more powerful than you might expect. You can confirm this by holding your breath after exhaling. In just a few seconds, your mind will grow restless as your urge to inhale rapidly intensifies.

This connection between mind and breath is fundamental to all *prānāyāma* techniques. An important application of this principle is to deliberately slow and deepen your breathing for the sake of quieting your mind. This particularly useful technique will be employed in the next exercise.

Breathing deeply is required in many kinds of *prānāyāma*. Normal breathing is usually rather shallow and is sometimes hindered by bad habits like slouching. We typically draw breath only into the upper parts of our chests, leaving the lower reaches of our lungs unfilled. To fill our lungs completely during *prāṇāyāma* requires extra effort to overcome the habit of shallow breathing.

To understand how to fill your lungs completely, imagine filling a pitcher with water: it is filled from the bottom up. In the same way, for *prāṇāyāma* you must fill your lungs from the bottom up. Begin each inhalation by breathing into your abdomen, allowing your belly to swell. Then fill the middle of your chest, letting your ribs expand. Finally, fill the top of your lungs as you complete the deep inhalation.

This method of filling your lungs from the bottom up is informally known as yogic breathing. When your lungs are completely filled, you bring more oxygen into your body with each breath. As a result, you need not breathe as frequently; you can comfortably breathe more slowly. Thus your breathing can simultaneously become deeper and slower, exerting a powerful calming effect on your mind.

The following meditation exercise presents a technique that slows your breathing by making each exhalation twice as long as each inhalation, while using yogic breathing to deepen your breath.

Exercise 2-3

Slow Deep Breathing

Preparation:

Following the steps in Exercise 1-1, sit with proper posture, close your eyes, make a *sankalpa* to set aside your concerns, and perform the progressive relaxation exercise.

Practice:

Begin by performing *prāna vīkshana* as described in Exercise 1-2. Trace the passage of air with each inhalation as you count 1.....2.....3..... and again trace the passage of air with each exhalation as you count 4.....5.....6..... Continue for several minutes before proceeding.

Next, using the yogic breathing technique described earlier, inhale deeply, filling your lungs from the bottom up, as you count 1.....2.....3..... Then exhale very slowly, gradually releasing the air from your lungs as you count twice as long, 1.....2.....3.....4.....5.....6..... Repeat this entire sequence.

Be sure to adjust your breathing so that you never feel lightheaded or short of breath. Continue for ten minutes or more.

Options:

Instead of counting to three as you inhale, mentally recite the word "peace" three times. And instead of counting to six as you exhale, mentally recite the word "release" three times. With each inhalation, imagine being increasingly filled with tranquility, peace, and well-being. With each exhalation, imagine letting go more and more completely of any remaining stress, tension, or anxiety.

Conclusion:

Stop counting and allow your breathing to return to normal. Observe how you feel for a few moments before slowly opening your eyes.

Ujjayī Prānāyāma—The Victorious Breath

Slow breathing and the relaxation associated with it can sometimes lead to drowsiness which is a major impediment for meditation. The ancient yogis understood this well and devised several effective methods to promote alertness. One of these techniques is *ujjayī prānāyāma. Ujjayī* literally means victorious. This technique can help you conquer the enemy of drowsiness.

Ujjayī prānāyāma is based on a principle also used in modern times by athletes preparing for competitions. You might have seen an athlete exhaling forcefully through tightly pursed lips. By forcing his breath through a constricted opening, he increases the pressure of air in his lungs and thereby drives more oxygen into his bloodstream. *Ujjayī prānāyāma* also increases the air pressure in the lungs. It does so not by exhaling through pursed lips but by exhaling with the air passage constricted at the larynx.

To learn this technique, you must first identify your larynx muscles. You can do this by simply clearing your throat. Your larynx muscles are constricted whenever you cough or clear your throat. If you constrict them tightly, you can completely close off the passage of air at the back of your throat. Try this for yourself now to become familiar with your larynx muscles.

Instead of completely closing the passage of air, if you constrict your larynx muscles slightly, you can partially close the air passage. This partial closure is required for *ujjayī pranāyāma*. In this technique, you force your breath through a narrowed passage in your throat to restrict its flow.

If you constrict your larynx muscles too much, you will make a snoring sound as you exhale which can irritate your throat (and anyone else nearby). If you fail to constrict these muscles sufficiently, your breath will flow without any restriction and all benefit will be lost. Proper constriction of your larynx muscles will partially restrict the flow of air and make a distinct hissing sound as you exhale.

You can learn this technique now by inhaling through your nose and then exhaling through your nose with your larynx muscles slightly constricted to partially restrict the passage of air. When you can produce a distinct hissing sound with each exhalation, you are constricting your larynx muscles properly.

In the practice of *ujjayī pranāyāma*, the passage of air is generally restricted during both inhalation and exhalation. But restricting the breath during inhalation might not be suitable for everyone, especially those new to *pranāyāma*. For this reason, the meditation exercise on the following page presents a modified form of *ujjayī pranāyāma* in which your breath is restricted only as you exhale.

Exercise 2-4

Ujjayī Prānāyāma

Preparation:

Following the steps in Exercise 1-1, sit with proper posture, close your eyes, make a *sankalpa* to set aside your concerns, and perform the progressive relaxation exercise.

Practice:

Begin by performing *prāna vīkshana* as described in Exercise 1-2. Trace the passage of air with each inhalation as you count 1.....2.....3..... and again trace the passage of air with each exhalation as you count 4.....5.....6..... Continue for several minutes before proceeding.

Next, stop counting and use the yogic breathing technique described before to inhale deeply, filling your lungs completely from the bottom up. Then, constrict your larynx muscles slightly and exhale slowly, listening for the hissing sound to confirm proper constriction. Repeat this sequence.

Continue to trace the passage of air with each breath. Be sure to adjust your breathing so that you never feel lightheaded or short of breath. If your mind starts to wander, resume counting. Continue for ten minutes or more.

Options:

To deepen your practice, inhale a bit more deeply and exhale a bit more slowly, pausing for a second or two with your lungs full before each exhalation. Be careful to avoid causing any discomfort or strain.

Conclusion:

Allow your larynx muscles to relax and breathe normally. Observe how you feel for a few moments before slowly opening your eyes.

Inner Source of Peace

The *prānāyāma* techniques in this chapter can help quiet your mind and allow peace to arise from within, from your true self, *ātmā*. Vedanta defines *ātmā* as *sat cit ānanda* which is usually translated as existence, consciousness, and bliss. However, it is impossible to fully and accurately render this profound Sanskrit maxim with three simple English words. Each of the terms convey sophisticated teachings that are thoroughly unfolded by the teachings of Vedanta. We can discuss them only briefly here.

Sat (existence) means that which exists without change in the past, present, and future. This term reveals that your true self, *ātmā*, is unborn, uncreated, eternal, and unchanging. Thus it is utterly unlike all worldly forms of existence. *Cit* (consciousness) reveals *ātmā* to be the consciousness by which you know all mental activities. It is the shining light of awareness that illumines each of your thoughts, perceptions, and emotions. By this unchanging consciousness, your ever-changing *vrittis* are made known to you.

Ānanda is usually translated as bliss. Unfortunately, bliss is an exceedingly poor choice of words. The word bliss denotes an ecstatic experience. Like all experiences, bliss comes and goes. Further, the experience of bliss is known by the unchanging consciousness which is your true self, *ātmā*. Since bliss is an experience, it cannot be *ātmā*, the essential nature of the experiencer.

Ānanda is better understood to be fullness, wholeness, or perfection. *Ānanda* reveals the vastness and limitlessness of *ātmā*. This meaning is conveyed in the Bhagavad Gita with a beautiful metaphor:

आपूर्यमाणमचलप्रतिष्ठं समुद्रमापः प्रविशन्ति यद्वत् ।

āpūryamānam acala-pratishtham samudram āpah pravishanti yadvat

It is like a vast ocean, constantly being filled by many rivers, yet never increasing in depth.

BG 2.70

Figuratively speaking, *ātmā* is an ocean of *ānanda* existing within you. It is a vast reservoir of peace, happiness, and contentment which is the true source of love and joy. When your heart is filled with the sacred waters of this reservoir, it is only natural to express your fullness as kindness, love, and compassion for others. All these are manifestations of *ānanda*.

Yet these cherished expressions of *ānanda* are all too often absent from our behavior. When we are tired, stressed, or merely distracted, we might not respond to others with the kindness and compassion they deserve. When we feel emotionally drained, it is difficult to care for others and give them our loving attention. As noted in the introduction, we can only give to others what we ourselves possess.

Fortunately, meditation provides an opportunity to dive into the inner ocean of *ānanda*, so to speak. In meditation, you can dip into that vast reservoir again and again to refresh yourself and refill your heart with kindness and compassion. You need only close your eyes and quiet your mind to immerse yourself in *ānanda*.

Diving into the Ocean of *Ānanda*

There is a type of *prānāyāma* that not only quiets your mind but also puts you in touch with your true, divine nature. This technique involves the use of a mantra recited in synchronization with your breathing. There are several such techniques that employ both *prānāyāma* and mantras. Among them, the technique described below is perhaps the best known. It is specifically intended to help you appreciate your inner divinity. It is meant to lead you to metaphorically plunge into the vast reservoir of peace and happiness within.

This technique uses the mantra, *so'ham*, which is derived from the Sanskrit pronouns *sah* – that and *aham* – I. *So'ham* literally means I am that. "That" refers to your inner divinity, your true self, *ātmā*, which is *sat cit ānanda*. Therefore, an expanded meaning of this mantra is "I am that inner divinity, *ātmā*, u nborn, uncreated, eternal consciousness, perfect, full and complete, the source of all peace and joy."

This mantra is usually combined with the *ujjayī prānāyāma* technique described earlier. The syllable *so* is mentally recited during inhalation and the syllable *ham* is recited during exhalation. You must learn and practice *ujjayī prānāyāma* first before performing the *so'ham* technique described in the following meditation exercise.

Exercise 2-5

So'ham Prānāyāma

Preparation:

Following the steps in Exercise 1-1, sit with proper post-ure, close your eyes, make a *sankalpa* to set aside your concerns, and perform the progressive relaxation exercise.

Practice:

Begin by practicing *ujjayī prānāyāma* as described in Exer-cise 2-4. Use yogic breathing to inhale deeply, then constrict your larynx muscles slightly and exhale slowly, listening for the hissing sound to confirm proper constriction. Continue for several minutes before proceeding.

Next, begin mentally reciting the mantra *so'ham* while you continue to practice *ujjayī prānāyāma*. With each inhalation, recite the syllable *so* and reflect on its meaning—the inner divinity, *ātmā*, the vast reservoir of peace and happiness within. With each exhalation, recite the syllable *ham* and imagine yourself merging with that inner divinity or diving into an ocean of *ānanda*. Continue for ten minutes or more.

Options:

To deepen your practice, inhale a bit more deeply and ex-hale a bit more slowly, pausing for a second or two with your lungs full before each exhalation. Be careful to avoid causing any discomfort or strain.

Conclusion:

Stop reciting the mantra. Allow your larynx muscles to re-lax and breathe normally. Observe how you feel for a few moments before slowly opening your eyes.

CHAPTER THREE

CONCENTRATION: FOCUSING YOUR MIND

The biggest challenge faced when learning to meditate is restraining your mind from wandering. Minds are subject to all kinds of distractions. At any moment, your efforts to meditate can get sidetracked when your mind goes astray and ends up meandering in a maze of thoughts and rumination. It is like making a wrong turn in a car and finding yourself far from your destination. Once you lose your way, it takes a while to get back on the right track.

To illustrate this, suppose you are meditating on your breathing and happen to hear your neighbor's car pull into the driveway next door. The following series of distractions could ensue:

Inhale....exhale....inhale....exhale.... [car door shuts] Sounds like my neighbor has returned from his vacation.

Inhale....exhale....inhale....exhale.... Before he left, he promised to return the ladder he borrowed from me.

Inhale....exhale....inhale.... He still hasn't returned the ladder. Come to think of it, he hasn't returned my garden shears or shovel either.

Exhale....inhale.... How inconsiderate! I am kind enough to lend things to him and he behaves like a thoughtless....

The above example actually shows two different sources of distraction; one is the sound of the car, the other is the movement of your own mind. Your mind and your senses both have the power to drag your attention away from meditation. Both have to be restrained.

Everyone is susceptible to distractions like these. It is the very nature of the mind to wander. In meditation workshops I have conducted, attendees often admitted, "Swamiji, I have a problem. Whenever I try to meditate, my mind wanders." They seemed embarrassed to say this and spoke softly so no one else could hear. Perhaps they assumed that none of the other attendees had this problem. They could not have been more wrong.

Regardless of intelligence and willpower, every mind is subject to wandering. In the Bhagavad Gita, Sri Krishna explains this to Arjuna:

यततो ह्यपि कौन्तेय पुरुषस्य विपश्चितः ।
इन्द्रियाणि प्रमाथीनि हरन्ति प्रसभं मनः ॥

*yatato hyapi kaunteya purushasya vipashcitah
indriyāni pramāthīni haranti prasabham manah*

O Arjuna, even though an intelligent person strives hard,
the restless senses can forcibly rob away one's mind.

BG 2.60

"Senses" here includes your mind in addition to your
powers of sight, hearing, taste, smell, and touch. Mind is called
antahkarana which means inner (*antah*) sense organ (*karana*). It is
also referred to as the sixth sense organ. In meditation, all six
senses must be restrained. They must be withdrawn from
every possible source of distraction. A vivid metaphor for such
withdrawal is found in the Gita shortly before the verse quoted
above:

यदा संहरते चायं कूर्मोऽङ्गानीव सर्वशः ।

yadā samharate cāyam kūrmo 'ngānīva sarvashah

...like a tortoise withdraws its limbs from all directions.

BG 2.58

The tortoise's legs and tail represent your five senses. Its
head represents your mind. In response to a threat, a tortoise
withdraws all six appendages into the safety of its shell.
Similarly, you must withdraw your senses and mind for
meditation. But how can you do that? Can you simply decide
to turn off your power of sight or hearing? If you could choose
to withdraw your power of sight, you could look at this book
with your eyes wide open without seeing a thing.

Yet under certain circumstances, you can indeed withdraw your senses. For example, suppose you were engrossed
in reading this book and someone happened to speak to you.
You might not hear a single word. If so, your power of hearing
was completely withdrawn, though not as a result of willfully
choosing not to hear. Your hearing was withdrawn by
intensely concentrating your attention on the book.

To understand this process better, note that the tortoise
gathers its limbs within its shell in order to withdraw them.

71

Similarly, by gathering your attention closely, as you do when concentrating on a book, your attention is simultaneously withdrawn from distractions. This process is described by Patanjali in the following *sutra*:

तत्प्रतिषेधार्थमेकतत्त्वाभ्यासः ॥

tat-pratishedhārtham eka-tattvābhyāsah

To remove those (distractions), concentrate on one thing.

YS 1.32

This is a fundamental principle of meditation—the way to withdraw your mind and senses from distractions is by concentrating your attention on just one thing, on an object of meditation.

Pratyāhāra and *Dhāranā*

The discussion above brings us to the next two limbs of yoga. After *yama, niyama, āsana,* and *prānāyāma,* the fifth and sixth limbs are *pratyāhāra*—sense withdrawal and *dhāranā*—concentration. Since withdrawal of the senses is accomplished by means of concentration, as we just saw, these two *angas* are like two sides of a coin, different yet inseparably connected.

A modern illustration will be helpful here. Suppose you have a flashlight with an adjustable lens. When you turn the lens in one direction, the flashlight casts a wide beam, illumining everything across a broad area before you. When you turn its lens the other way, the flashlight casts a narrow, highly focused beam that illumines only one small spot. The following illustrations show how wide and narrow beams illumine an object on a stone patio very differently.

Illumination with Wide Beam

Illumination with Narrow Beam

The wide beam represents your attention through most of each day. Your mind has the capacity to be aware of a wide range of things simultaneously. This faculty is especially useful in activities like driving when you must be constantly aware of vehicles in front of you, beside you, and behind you as well.

When the flashlight's beam is narrowed, it illumines only one object. Everything outside the beam is plunged into darkness. The narrow beam represents your attention when you concentrate on something like reading a book. When your attention is sufficiently concentrated on one thing, everything else is ignored and distractions fade away.

Like the flashlight, your power of attention is adjustable; it can be wide or narrow. Of course, it is much easier to twist the lens of a flashlight than to narrowly focus your attention. The flashlight has one more advantage: after being adjusted, its beam remains narrow and needs no further adjustment. Your concentration, on the other hand, can weaken after a while and requires constant effort to maintain it. To keep your attention firmly concentrated may be difficult at first, but you can gradually develop the ability to maintain its narrow focus for longer and longer periods.

Concentration is an indispensable skill for meditation. As discussed in the introduction, this skill is learned like any other—with proper guidance and adequate practice. Proper guidance is provided by the meditation exercises later in this chapter. The necessary practice can be gained by following a simple principle whenever you meditate—each time your mind wanders away, gently bring it back. Bringing your mind back again and again is the primary means for developing your power of concentration.

Learning to meditate is a lot like learning to ride a bicycle. The first time you got on a bike, you promptly fell off. After getting back on, you fell off again. But before long, you were able to ride without difficulty. The same process occurs when you learn to meditate. You begin by focusing your attention on the object of meditation. Before long, your mind will wander, like falling off your bike. Then, you bring your mind back to the object, like getting back on your bike.

Each time your mind wanders, you must bring it back, again and again, as often as necessary. This instruction is given in the following verse from the Bhagavad Gita:

यतो यतो निश्चलति मनश्चञ्चलमस्थिरम् ।
ततस्ततो नियम्यैतदात्मन्येव वशं नयेत् ॥

yato yato nishcalati manash cancalam asthiram
tatas tato niyamyaitad ātmanyeva vasham nayet

Wherever your erratic, unstable mind wanders,
bring it back, again and again. Make it remain within.

BG 6.26

In a manner of speaking, you learned to ride a bicycle by getting back on each time you fell off. In the same way, you learn to concentrate your attention by bringing your mind back each time it wanders.

It is important not to criticize yourself when your mind wanders. After all, it is perfectly natural for your attention to stray now and then. Also, self-criticism can lead to frustration and tension which are counterproductive for meditation. So each time your mind wanders, you must bring it back gently, without harshness or self-criticism. And with practice, just as you became a skillful bike-rider, you can become a skillful meditator.

Object of Meditation

For *dhāranā*, concentration, your attention must be focused upon an appropriate object of meditation. This is stated by Patanjali in the following *sutra*:

देशबन्धश्चित्तस्य धारणा ॥

desha-bandhash cittasya dhāranā

Placing your mind (on an object of meditation) is *dhāranā*.

YS 3.1

Many kinds of objects are suitable for meditation, including sacred images, sounds, mantras, and so on. But when you first learn to concentrate your attention, it is best to choose something easy to grasp. In general, it is helpful to start with tangible things like forms, sounds, and sensations. You can later proceed to more subtle things like mental images and mantras.

The following three meditation exercises form a sequence using objects of meditation that progress step by step from the tangible towards the subtle. The first of these techniques is called *trātaka* or yogic gazing. Traditional manuals on *hatha* yoga prescribe gazing at an object without blinking until your eyes water. This is done for the sake of cleansing your eyes. The following exercise employs a less arduous form of this technique which is intended to train your mind rather than cleanse your eyes.

You must first choose a suitable article to gaze upon. Good choices include a lamp or candle flame, a picture or form of a deity, or a sacred symbol like a *mandala* or a depiction of *om*. Such objects should preferably be placed on an altar in a special location set aside for prayer and meditation.

Exercise 3-1

Trāṭaka – Yogic Gazing

Preparation:

Following the steps in Exercise 1-1, sit with proper posture, close your eyes, make a *sankalpa* to set aside your concerns, and perform the progressive relaxation exercise.

Practice:

Open your eyes and gently gaze at your chosen object. Blink normally to avoid burning or watering eyes. Focus your attention on the image before you—its shape, features, color, texture, etc. Avoid making mental comments about the object; simply appreciate its appearance without words.

If your mind wanders or if you start mentally commenting on the object, gently bring your mind back and focus it on the object once again. Continue for ten minutes or more.

Options:

After several minutes of gazing at the object, close your eyes and focus your attention on its image in your mind. Use your imagination to envision the object as vividly as possible. If the image fades or if your mind wanders, open your eyes and return to gazing upon the physical object.

The next meditation exercise introduces a technique called *bhramarī* which literally means a bee. *Bhramarī* is a form of *prāṇāyāma* in which you hum or make a buzzing sound with your voice as you exhale through your nose. This buzzing sound becomes the object of meditation on which you focus your attention. Traditional manuals on *hatha* yoga prescribe using your fingers and thumbs to close your eyes and ears during this practice. The following exercise omits that aspect since its main intent is to train your mind to concentrate.

Exercise 3-2

Bhramarī Prānāyāma

Preparation:

Following the steps in Exercise 1-1, sit with proper posture, close your eyes, make a *sankalpa* to set aside your concerns, and perform the progressive relaxation exercise.

Practice:

Inhale deeply through your nose using the yogic breathing technique described in the previous chapter. Then, keeping your mouth closed, make a humming sound as you exhale through your nose, imagining that you are chanting *om*. Repeat this sequence.

Concentrate your attention on the buzzing sound. If your mind wanders, gently bring it back to the sound. Be sure to adjust your breathing so that you never become lightheaded or short of breath. Continue for ten minutes or more.

Options:

To deepen your practice, pause for a second or two with your lungs full before exhaling with the buzzing sound. Be sure the pause produces no discomfort or strain.

The next meditation exercise employs constriction of your larynx muscles as in *ujjayī prānāyāma,* described in Exercise 2-4. In this exercise, however, rather than focusing your attention on your breath, you will focus on the sounds produced by your breathing. As you inhale using the yogic breathing technique described in the last chapter, you can hear the air as it enters your nostrils. During exhalation with the constriction of your larynx muscles, you can hear the hissing sound as the air escapes from your throat. Direct your attention towards these sounds which are the objects of meditation for this technique.

Exercise 3-3

Concentration on Breath Sounds

Preparation:

Following the steps in Exercise 1-1, sit with proper posture, close your eyes, make a *sankalpa* to set aside your concerns, and perform the progressive relaxation exercise.

Practice:

Inhale deeply using the yogic breathing technique, filling your lungs completely from the bottom up, and directing your attention towards the sound of air entering your nostrils. Then exhale slowly, with a slight constriction of your larynx muscles, directing your attention towards the hissing sound of air escaping from your throat. Repeat this sequence.

Be sure to adjust your breathing so that you never feel lightheaded or short of breath. Continue for ten minutes or more.

Options:

To deepen your practice, pause for a second or two with your lungs full before you exhale. Be sure the pause produces no discomfort or strain.

Conclusion:

Allow your larynx muscles to relax and breathe normally. Observe how you feel for a few moments before slowly opening your eyes.

Developing Your Power of Concentration

There is a delightful story, passed down for generations, that describes how concentration is produced in meditation. The story refers to the trained elephants which have long been used in India to assist in heavy work like moving boulders or felled trees. Even today you can see elephants working on construction sites in rural parts of the country.

Suppose an elephant is led by its trainer, the mahout, through a small town on the way to a construction site. In the middle of the town is a bazaar where both sides of the road are lined with handcarts, each piled high with fruits and vegetables. As the elephant is led down the narrow lane, it is likely to spot a bunch of bananas and reach out with its trunk to snatch them. The mahout must prevent such a theft from occurring because he would have to pay for any bananas devoured by his elephant.

The mahout must restrain the elephant's powerful trunk from wandering, just as you must restrain your powerful mind. If the mahout were to catch hold of the elephant's trunk, he would easily be overpowered. In the same way, if you try to coerce your mind into a state of silent submission, you will probably be overpowered, as discussed in the prior chapter.

To avoid any problems, the mahout gives his elephant a stick to carry before entering the bazaar. The elephant grasps the stick with its nimble trunk and walks down the narrow lane. When the elephant spies some bananas, it is unable to grab them as long as it holds on to the stick. And because the elephant has been well trained by the mahout, it will not drop the stick.

The stick serves to preoccupy the elephant's powerful trunk and thus restrains its tendency to wander and cause mischief. In the same way, focusing your attention on an object of meditation preoccupies your mind and keeps it from wandering. In the prior exercises, several such objects of meditation were introduced, including a candle flame, humming sound, and your breath. As long as you hold on to an object like these by fixing your attention on it, the tendency of your mind to wander will be restrained.

However, the elephant seems to be better trained than we are. The elephant will grasp a stick firmly whereas we are likely to drop an object of meditation repeatedly, especially when we first learn to meditate. It takes much practice before our attention can be constantly focused on an object of meditation without being interrupted by distractions.

When an elephant first begins its training, it may drop the stick again and again. Each time, the mahout patiently gives the stick back to the elephant to try again. In the same way, an untrained mind will drop the object of meditation repeatedly. But you can train your mind by gently bringing it back each time it wanders. In weight lifting, each repetition of an exercise makes your muscles stronger. In meditation, each time you bring your attention back, your power of concentration grows stronger.

In the next exercise, the mantra *om* serves as the object of meditation upon which you will fix your attention. *Om* is not a word; it is a sound that symbolically represents God or Ishvara, the Supreme Being. *Om* is an ideal sound-symbol for Ishvara because it includes all other sounds. When you chant *om*, the sound begins in your abdomen and ends at your lips, thereby involving your entire vocal apparatus — lungs, trachea, larynx, throat, and mouth. Because uttering *om* involves your whole vocal system, it is considered a complete, all-inclusive sound suitable for representing the supreme source of all.

The following meditation exercise combines chanting *om* aloud with a simple *prānāyāma* technique. The inclusion of *prānāyāma* will help calm your mind and reduce its tendency to wander. Focus your attention on the sound of *om* resonating in each part of your vocal apparatus as you chant aloud.

Exercise 3-4

Om with *Prānāyāma*

Preparation:

Following the steps in Exercise 1-1, sit with proper posture, close your eyes, make a *sankalpa* to set aside your concerns, and perform the progressive relaxation exercise.

Practice:

Using the yogic breathing technique, inhale deeply through your nose, filling your lungs completely from the bottom up. Then chant the mantra *om* aloud as you exhale, extending its length as much as possible: *ooooooooooommm*. With a sufficiently deep inhalation, you can probably sustain the sound for five seconds or more. Repeat this sequence.

Concentrate on the sound of *om* and gently bring your attention back to the sound if your mind wanders. Be sure to adjust your breathing so that you never feel lightheaded or short of breath. Continue for ten minutes or more.

Options:

To deepen your practice, pause for a second or two with your lungs full before you chant *om*. Be sure the pause produces no discomfort or strain.

Conclusion:

Stop chanting and breathe normally. Observe how you feel for a few moments before slowly opening your eyes.

Associative Thinking

With the help of the prior meditation exercises, you may have discovered the wonderful sense of stillness that arises as your mind begins to quiet down. Throughout the day, your mind is generally filled with non-stop chatter—thinking, planning, worrying, and so on. Compared to that chatter, the calm of meditation can come as a great relief. Suppose you have been stuck for hours near a clattering machine or blaring television. When the noise finally stops, you can suddenly feel enveloped by a blanket of blissful silence. The experience is much the same when relentless mental chatter stops completely and your mind finally comes to rest.

Our minds are often caught up in a steady stream of thoughts continually flowing from one topic to another. Psychologists call this associative thinking because each thought has a connection or association that links it to the next thought. Associative thinking often guides casual conversation when it drifts effortlessly from one subject to another.

Because we are so accustomed to associative thinking, we can easily drift away into a meandering stream of thoughts, even during meditation practice. Such was the problem for the meditator at the beginning of this chapter who was distracted by the sound of a car pulling into the driveway. A chain of associated thoughts developed as follows:

Car sound → links to neighbor.

Neighbor → links to promise to return the ladder.

Ladder → links to other items not returned.

Other items → links to annoyance.

In this example, each thought is linked to the next thought, creating a chain of associative thinking. We can spend much of each day with our minds ensnared in long chains of thought. Such is the nature of the mind.

How can we break free from these chains of thought? Once started, they are difficult to break because the associations linking one thought to the next are quite strong. Instead of trying to break these chains, it is easier to redirect them, to turn them towards more desirable paths. We can actually harness the mind's tendency for associative thinking as an aid to meditation, as will be explained below.

Let us examine how associative thinking affects meditation. The meditator's chain of distracting thoughts about his neighbor could be represented as:

$$A \rightarrow B \rightarrow C \rightarrow D$$

Suppose this sequence was replaced by a different chain of thoughts, a chain of identical thoughts such as:

$$A \rightarrow A \rightarrow A \rightarrow A$$

This is exactly what happens in meditation: a series of wandering thoughts is replaced by a series of identical thoughts fixed on an object of meditation. For example, in the prior exercise, the object of meditation was the mantra *om*.

When practicing that exercise, the following chain of thoughts will be produced:

$$om \rightarrow om \rightarrow om \rightarrow om \rightarrow om$$

Each *om* links to another *om*, which helps keep your mind from wandering. The use of a mantra replaces a chain of wandering thoughts with a chain of mantras. In this way, your mind's tendency for associative thinking can be harnessed for meditation. Much more about the use of mantras will be discussed in the next chapter.

Walking and Associative Thinking

If you take a leisurely walk with a friend, it is easy to get engrossed in nonstop chitchat about everything and anything. As we have seen, this kind of rambling conversation is the result of associative thinking. Even if you walk alone, you can easily get absorbed in your own chains of thought. When you get caught up in associative thinking in this way, it is possible to walk through a charming park or picturesque spot without really experiencing the beauty that surrounds you.

Natural beauty is hard to appreciate when you are looking through a thick veil of thoughts. Associative thinking is like a blanket of words that surrounds you and obscures your view. It dulls your senses and blunts everything you experience.

Fortunately, this veil of thoughts can be removed by a specific meditation technique. Instead of focusing your attention on an object of meditation, it can be focused on the beauty around you. You can direct your attention towards whatever you perceive, all that you see, hear, taste, smell, and touch. Focusing your attention on your five senses helps you resist the tendency for associative thinking. It also helps you observe and appreciate the beauty that surrounds you.

The exercise below provides instructions for a contemplative walk in which you remove the veil of thoughts to more fully appreciate the beauty of nature.

Exercise 3-5

Contemplative Nature Walk

Preparation:

Go to a beautiful place suitable for walking. Make a *sankalpa* to set aside your problems and concerns as in Exercise 1-1. If you are accompanied by someone, agree to remain silent for the duration of the walk.

Practice:

Choose a particular sense and focus your attention on those sensations alone. For example, take the sense of sight and focus your attention exclusively on the various colors, shapes, shadows, and textures you perceive. Try to avoid mental comments like "What a beautiful flower." Simply appreciate the beauty around you through your senses without words.

After a while, turn to your sense of hearing and focus your attention on sounds—birds chirping, leaves rustling, wind sighing, gentle footsteps, etc. As before, avoid mental comments.

Then turn to smells like the fragrance of flowers and the rich smell of earth. Next, turn to your sense of touch and feel with your fingers the texture of leaves, bark, flower petals, rocks, etc. Feel the warm sun and gentle breeze on your skin.

You may shift from one sense to another as you like, but be sure to pick one at a time to help keep your attention narrowly focused. Throughout your walk, avoid making mental comments about anything you experience.

CHAPTER FOUR

MANTRA JAPA

Of the many suitable objects of meditation, mantras are probably used more extensively than any other. Mantras are invocations, mostly in Sanskrit, which are repeated mentally for meditation. Mantra *japa*, recitation of mantras, is perhaps the most widely used meditation technique in the Hindu tradition. It is so popular because it is powerful and versatile yet simple to practice. Thus it is an ideal technique for beginners and advanced meditators alike.

The meaning of the word mantra is traditionally defined as *manas trāyate*, that which releases or liberates (*trayate*) the mind (*manas*) from its troubles and limitations. It can also be derived from the verbal root *man*, to think, with the agent affix, *tr*. This derivation denotes a tool or instrument for the mind. Therefore a mantra can be considered an instrument of concentration or a tool for focusing your attention.

The purpose of focusing your attention on a mantra or any other object of meditation is to reach the seventh of yoga's eight limbs, *dhyāna*. *Dhyāna* simply means meditation. In Patanjali's system, it follows *dhāranā* — concentration and prepares you for the final limb, *samādhi* — absorption. Patanjali defines *dhyāna* in the following *sutra*:

तत्र प्रत्ययैकतानता ध्यानम् ॥

tatra pratyayaika-tānatā dhyānam

There (regarding the object of meditation)
a stream of identical thoughts is *dhyāna*.

YS 3.2

Dhyāna is a stream of identical thoughts fixed on an object of meditation. It is a chain of thoughts, a chain of identical *vritti*s uninterrupted by any extraneous thoughts. When meditating on a mantra, all mental activities are exclusively directed towards the mantra during the state of *dhyāna*.

Another traditional definition of *dhyāna* is *sajātīya-vritti-pravāha*, a flow (*pravāha*) of identical (*sajātīya*) thoughts (*vritti*). A striking metaphor is used to depict this condition. As viscous oil is slowly poured from a vessel, it forms a delicate ribbon of liquid. If the vessel is held perfectly still, the steady flow of oil appears motionless, like a solid ribbon of liquid suspended in space. Even as it flows, the oil seems perfectly still.

In the same way, when a perfectly steady stream of *vritti*s flows in your mind, you can experience absolute stillness. That is *dhyāna*, a state of stillness arising from an unwavering flow of identical *vritti*s. In the practice of mantra *japa*, *dhyāna* is achieved when your attention is fixed on a stream of identical mantras which flow without any interruption or deviation whatsoever.

Choice of Mantras

"Which is the best mantra?" is a question frequently asked. If there was a particular mantra whose power and efficacy were greater than any other, this question could be answered briefly. But there is no best mantra. On the other hand, there are ancient Vedic mantras, mantras from the Puranas and Mahabharata, mantras to various deities, long and short mantras, mantras incorporating sacred sounds, and mantras invoking each of the thousands of names for God.

Though none of these mantras could be considered best, each has its unique qualities. To explore the relative merits of various mantras, let us return to the elephant story from the prior chapter. In that story, a stick is given to an elephant to restrain its trunk from wandering. In this metaphor, the stick represents a mantra.

Now, what kind of stick should the mahout give to his elephant to carry? He could give it a nicely carved piece of sandalwood, or even an elegant silver-plated stick. Yet neither would restrain the elephant's trunk any better than an ordinary stick picked up from the roadside. To the elephant, the particular kind of stick makes no difference; it has no preference. The mahout, on the other hand, would probably choose the valuable silver-plated stick if he were given a choice.

The choice of sticks represents our freedom to choose one mantra or another. If our minds were like the well-trained elephant, choosing a mantra would be needless; all would work equally well. But as discussed in the last chapter, our minds are not like an elephant. We are more like the mahout. We are naturally inclined to choose whatever is most valuable. And the more valuable something is, the more tightly we will hold on to it. For this reason, a mantra of great value will hold our attention better than one of little or no value. Therefore, we must discover the value of a mantra before it can fully command our attention.

What is it that determines a mantra's value? There are several factors, but the most important of them is *your attitude*. A mantra's value largely depends on your own estimation of it. To misquote an old adage, "Value is in the eye of the beholder." One person might see an old table as being a rickety piece of junk, while another might see it as a valuable antique. The actual value of the table must be discovered. Likewise, a meditator must personally discover the value of a mantra.

To better appreciate this principle, consider the story about a young student who approached a guru and asked to be given a mantra. The guru said, "Come back next month." A month later, the student returned but the guru again said, "Come back next month." Each time the student returned, he was told to wait one more month. After twelve long years had elapsed in this way, the guru finally gave him a mantra.

Why did the guru wait so long? If a mantra was imparted immediately, the young, immature student might have considered it ordinary, easily obtained, and therefore of little value. With such an attitude, he might have found it difficult to concentrate on the mantra, however powerful it might have been. But because he had to wait, his enthusiasm and dedication grew strong. He considered his long-awaited mantra to be a precious treasure. Due to his great value for the mantra, it could command his full attention in meditation, even if it happened to be the most commonplace of mantras.

From this story, it is clear that your attitude affects the efficacy of a mantra. Another illustration of this principle is found in a few organizations that charge a fee for receiving a mantra. This approach is strongly frowned upon by traditional gurus, so why would some groups use it? Perhaps they are guided by a familiar Western maxim, "You get what you pay for." A mantra that is given freely might be considered worthless. But meditators who must pay for a mantra might value it more greatly and be more committed to using it regularly.

Charging a fee or making someone wait twelve years are methods of instilling greater value in meditators for their mantras. However, most gurus find no need for all this. Such approaches are unnecessary if the guru who imparts a mantra also helps his student discover the mantra's true value, the value that stems from its inherent power—its *shakti*.

Mantra *Shakti*

Traditional mantras are immensely valuable because they possess a unique capacity to draw our full attention during meditation. That capacity is the mantra's *shakti*, its power. The *shakti* of a mantra derives from several sources. First of all, mantras are prayers. Most of them are Sanskrit invocations addressed to various aspects of Ishvara. Any form of prayer connects us to a power infinitely greater than ourselves. That infinite power is invoked when a mantra is recited, just as it is in prayer. Thus the prayerful dimension of mantras is an important source of their *shakti*.

A number of unconventional, non-traditional mantras have been composed in modern times. Various words and sounds have been promoted for use in meditation. Some of these sounds are actually described as being meaningless syllables. While it is certainly possible to focus your attention on such mantras, they lack the prayerful meaning and inherent *shakti* of traditional mantras.

In his *sutra*s, Patanjali prescribes that a mantra's meaning should be contemplated upon during mantra *japa*:

तज्जपस्तदर्थभावनम् ॥

taj-japas tad-artha-bhāvanam

Repeat that (mantra) and contemplate its meaning.

YS 1.28

Traditional mantras, as prayers invoking various aspects of Ishvara, have meanings worthy of deep contemplation. Yet some meditators fail to understand the meaning of their mantras. To recite a prayer or mantra without comprehension weakens its power and can lead to mindless, mechanical repetition. Fortunately, this problem is easily rectified; most mantras are not difficult to understand. In Appendix A, you will find many mantras with explanations of their meanings and related symbolism.

Most mantras share a common pattern or formula. They usually begin with *om*, a sound-symbol that represents Ishvara, as explained before. Many mantras also include the word *namah* which is generally translated as salutations. It is derived from the root *nam* which means to bend or bow. Therefore, *namah* suggests bowing in reverence, obeisance, or surrender.

Due to rules of grammar, *namah* sometimes becomes *namo*, *namas*, or *nama*, depending on the word which follows it.

The most important word in any mantra is a name of Ishvara, a name for one of the many forms in which God is worshiped. When *namah* is present, that name is grammatically inflected to mean unto Ishvara. For example, *om namah shivāya* means salutations or obeisance unto Shiva. *Om namo nārāyānāya* means salutations unto Narayana, unto Vishnu. Any of the thousands of names for Ishvara can be used in a mantra.

Most mantras are relatively short. Some are just three words long, as in the examples above. Other mantras, like the well-known Gayatri Mantra, are greater in length. Mantras of all lengths are effective, but for novice meditators, short mantras may be easier to use. Yet the value of longer mantras should not be underestimated. They may be more difficult to use initially, but their complexity demands more attention which can help prevent your mind from wandering. The mantra *om* alone is generally not recommended for mantra *japa*. Because it is so short, your mind can easily slip away from it.

Many mantras include one or more sound-symbols known as *bījākshara*s or seed (*bīja*) syllables (*akshara*). These are typically one-syllable sounds like *shrīm*, *hrīm*, and *aim*. The sound-syllable *om* is also a *bījākshara*. Seed syllables are sometimes associated with particular deities. For example, *shrīm* often represents Lakshmi, goddess of wealth, and *aim* is often used for Sarasvati, goddess of knowledge. A number of mantras that include *bījākshara*s can be found in Appendix A.

A mantra's *shakti* stems not only from its meaning as a prayer, but also from the very sounds of its Sanskrit words. Sanskrit is called *deva bhāshā*, language of the gods. It is held to be of divine origin, revealed to the ancient *rishi*s along with the holy Vedic scriptures which are the first compositions in Sanskrit. Thus every syllable of the language is believed to be sacred. For this reason, Sanskrit mantras are revered as divine sounds.

Even if you do not ascribe to this belief, Sanskrit is indeed an extraordinary language. The word *samskrita* itself means refined or perfected. Sanskrit is an ancient, scriptural language derived from no other tongues. It is endowed with a precise method of pronunciation, a vast vocabulary, and an unusually sophisticated grammar. These qualities make Sanskrit unparalleled among the world's languages.

Practice of Mantra *Japa*

From the discussion above, it is clear that mantras are ideal for use as objects of meditation. Their sounds, meanings, and inherent *shakti* all help draw your attention, making it easier to concentrate on the mantra. An additional technique that helps restrain your mind from wandering during mantra *japa* will be explained in the coming paragraphs.

Let us return to the bicycle metaphor from the previous chapter. Just as you learn to ride a bike by getting back on each time you fall, so too, you learn to meditate by bringing your attention back each time it wanders. Nowadays, parents often install training wheels on their children's bicycles to help prevent frequent falls. Is there an equivalent to training wheels for the practice of mantra *japa*? Indeed there is: chanting your mantra aloud. Chanting aloud keeps your mind fixed on a mantra just like training wheels keep children upright on their bikes.

Mantra *japa* is traditionally divided into three types or levels:

1) *vaikharī* – chanting aloud
2) *upāmshu* – whispering or moving ones lips
3) *mānasika* – mental recitation

Vaikharī japa, chanting a mantra aloud, helps like training wheels on a child's bicycle.

As children learn to ride, the training wheels that had once been so helpful soon become awkward encumbrances that need to be removed. In the same way, chanting aloud may be helpful at first, but the extra effort required eventually becomes a hindrance. When this happens, you can shift to *upāmshu japa* in which you whisper your mantra or simply move your lips as you chant mentally. Sooner or later, this too may feel cumbersome. Then you are ready for *mānasika japa*, purely mental recitation.

For the following meditation exercises, you will need a mantra. If you already have one, you may continue to use it. Otherwise, you may choose a mantra from Appendix A. If you are just learning to meditate, select one from the section, "Mantras for Beginners." If you usually pray to a particular form of Ishvara, it might be helpful to choose a mantra addressed to that deity.

Exercise 4-1

Three-Level Mantra *Japa*

Preparation:

Following the steps in Exercise 1-1, sit with proper posture, close your eyes, make a *sankalpa* to set aside your concerns, and perform the progressive relaxation exercise.

Practice – Part 1:

Begin by reciting your mantra aloud, chanting it with a soft voice. Focus your attention on the sound and meaning of the mantra. As soon as your mind has settled down and is fixed on the mantra without wandering, proceed to Part 2.

Practice – Part 2:

Instead of chanting aloud, whisper your mantra or recite it silently while moving your lips. When your mind wanders, gently bring it back to the mantra. When your mind remains fixed on the mantra without wandering, proceed to Part 3.

Practice – Part 3:

Recite your mantra silently without moving your lips. When your mind wanders, gently bring it back to the mantra. Continue for ten minutes or more.

Options:

If your mind wanders excessively in Part 2 or 3, return to the previous level and continue your practice.

Managing a Wandering Mind

If your mind still wanders a lot during meditation, even after practicing each of the exercises in this book so far, do not be discouraged. Training the mind is an exceedingly challenging task. If you find yourself struggling with this, you are in good company—even Arjuna, the mighty warrior, struggled to control his mind. In the sixth chapter of the Bhagavad Gita where Sri Krishna teaches Arjuna how to meditate, Arjuna expressed his great frustration in the following verse:

चञ्चलं हि मनः कृष्ण प्रमाथि बलवद् दृढम् ।
तस्याहं निग्रहं मन्ये वायोरिव सुदुष्करम् ॥

cancalam hi manah krishna pramāthi balavad dridham
tasyāham nigraham manye vāyor iva sudushkaram

O Krishna, my mind wanders constantly, as if agitated by force.
I consider it as hard to restrain as trying to stop the wind.

BG 6.34

It is remarkable that Arjuna voices this complaint not at the beginning of the chapter but towards its end, after Sri Krishna has already explained in detail how to restrain a wandering mind. In spite of these extensive teachings, Arjuna was still perplexed. Such is the challenge of controlling a mind which is as fickle as the wind!

If the challenge is so great, how can we even hope to control our minds? The answer is found in the very next verse where Sri Krishna responds to Arjuna's frustration with these comforting and very practical words of advice :

असंशयं महाबाहो मनो दर्निग्रहं चलम् ।
अभ्यासेन तु कौन्तेय वैराग्येण च गृह्यते ॥

asamshayam mahābāho mano durnigraham calam
abhyāsena tu kaunteya vairāgyena ca grihyate

O Arjuna, the mind is certainly fickle and hard to control.
But with practice and dispassion, it can be restrained.

BG 6.35

Practice and dispassion, *abhyāsa* and *vairāgya*, are the primary means for training your mind. The need for practice is obvious from earlier discussions. But how does dispassion help?

When your mind wanders repeatedly in spite of considerable efforts to restrain it, you might eventually become disappointed, frustrated, or even angry with yourself. Emotional reactions like these can undermine your attempts to meditate. Disappointment can rob your enthusiasm. Frustration and anger can create agitation and make your mind even harder to control.

Vairāgya or dispassion means to be detached from the results of your efforts. Such detachment implies being free from expectations. When you have no particular expectations, you can accept the results of your efforts—desirable or undesirable—with equanimity. And with equanimity, you can remain patiently committed to your practice, whether your mind cooperates or not, without feeling disappointed or frustrated.

Abhyāsa and *vairāgya*, practice and dispassion, are crucial for training your mind. Not surprisingly, Patanjali uses the very same two words to explain how your mind can be restrained from wandering:

अभ्यासवैराग्याभ्यां तन्निरोधः ॥

abhyāsa-vairāgyābhyām tan-nirodhah

Through practice and dispassion, that (wandering) will cease.

YS 1.12

During meditation, these two directives are to be followed meticulously. Every time your mind wanders, bring it back immediately, without harboring any self-criticism, disappointment, or frustration. Herein lies the secret to training your mind. Actually, it is no secret; *abhyāsa* and *vairāgya* have been clearly prescribed in the Bhagavad Gita, Yoga Sutras, and other texts on meditation.

Aids for Mantra *Japa*

Mantra *japa* is generally done silently, although it can be helpful to chant aloud at first as discussed before. When chanting silently, your mind will naturally be more susceptible to distractions. There are several ways to minimize this problem. One way is to recite your mantra more rapidly when your mind begins to wander. By speeding up, your attention will become more intensely focused. After a minute or so, you can return to your normal speed. Another method is to recite the mantra more loudly or forcefully in your mind. This is done by simply imagining the voice in your mind to get louder. After your attention is again fixed on the mantra, you can return to your normal level.

If these techniques are unable to keep your mind from wandering excessively, you might find it helpful to listen to an audio recording of mantra chanting while you meditate. A wide variety of commercial recordings are available in which various mantras are chanted or sung with different melodies. You can also find a number of my own recordings freely available on our ashram's website. Please see Appendix B for further information.

There is nothing wrong with using a recording while you meditate, but to do so indefinitely is like keeping training wheels on an eleven-year-old's bicycle. It is desirable to outgrow the need for recordings. A good way to transition from using a recording to meditating in silence is to mentally chant the mantra with the same melody as the recording. Just as you can sing a song in your mind, you can mentally chant a mantra with a melody you enjoy.

Exercise 4-2

Silent Mantra *Japa*

Preparation:

Following the steps in Exercise 1-1, sit with proper posture, close your eyes, make a *sankalpa* to set aside your concerns, and perform the progressive relaxation exercise.

Practice:

Begin reciting your mantra mentally. If it is helpful, you may chant it silently with a favorite melody. Focus your attention on the sound and meaning of the mantra.

When your mind wanders, gently bring it back to the mantra without self-criticism, letting go of any disappointment or frustration. Continue for ten minutes or more.

Options:

If your mind wanders excessively, try reciting the mantra more rapidly or more loudly in your mind. After your attention is again fixed on the mantra, resume your recitation as before.

Using a *Japa Mālā*

Another technique that helps prevent your mind from wandering is to use a *japa mālā*. A *japa mālā* is a circular string of beads which is slowly turned by hand, one bead for each mantra. The physical act of turning the beads and the tactile sense of the beads in your hand help keep your attention firmly focused on your mantra.

*Japa mālā*s are usually 108 beads long. 108 is a number that symbolically represents completeness. An additional bead, called *meru*, is attached to the *mālā* to indicate its beginning and end. Shorter *mālās* generally consist of 54 beads and also include an extra *meru* bead. The beads are usually one of several types such as *rudrāksha* seeds, round crystals with smooth or faceted surfaces, or wooden beads carved from tulasi, rose, or sandalwood. Some types are traditionally associated with a particular deity. For example, *rudrāksha* seeds are associated with Shiva and tulasi beads with forms of Vishnu. Such customs need not be followed rigidly; any *mālā* can be used for mantra *japa*.

There are several conventions regarding the proper use of a *mālā*. The most widely used method is described in the following exercise.

Exercise 4-3

How to Use a *Japa Mālā*

In your right hand, drape the *mālā* over your middle finger, holding your index finger away, as the illustration shows. Do not let the hanging beads touch the floor or your feet.

Position the *mālā* so that the first bead next to the *meru* bead (1) is held between your thumb and the side of your middle finger. Recite your mantra once. Then pull the bead towards you with your thumb until the second bead (2) rests on your middle finger. Put your thumb on that bead and recite the mantra again. Continue in this manner with your eyes closed, relying on your sense of touch to navigate your way around the *mālā*.

You will know that you have completed the entire *mālā* when you reach the *meru* bead again. If you want to continue, it is customary to avoid crossing the *meru* bead. Instead, turn the *mālā* completely around in your hand and proceed in the reverse direction.

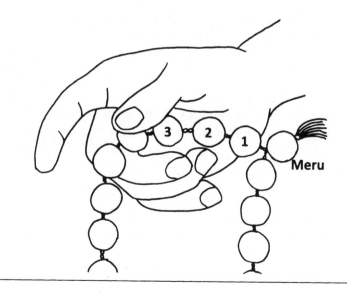

Dangers of Mechanical Recitation

A number of meditators have approached me with virtually identical problems regarding their practice of mantra *japa*. They meditated each morning, reciting their mantras 108 times while using a *japa mālā*. But as they recited their mantras, they simultaneously thought about other matters, such as what chores and errands needed to be done later in the day.

How could their minds wander like that even while reciting their mantras? Mantra *japa* can gradually become so mindless or mechanical that it can be done automatically, with minimal effort and attention. It then becomes possible to think about other things at the same time. Our minds are capable of multitasking. They can easily do two or more things simultaneously, like taking notes while listening to a lecture. This is something quite useful. However, our capacity for multitasking becomes a liability during meditation if our attention becomes split between mantra *japa* and other activities.

Meditation requires our full attention, not some fraction of it. The above problem can be avoided if we are diligent in bringing our attention back to the mantra as soon as it begins to wander. Unfortunately, some meditators fail to make that effort consistently. They sometimes allow their minds to wander during mantra *japa*, without exercising any restraint.

This lapse of discipline soon becomes habitual; their minds grow accustomed to wandering during meditation.

This problem can be prevented by following two simple rules. First, every time your mind wanders, bring it back at once. Second, if you become weary of bringing your mind back and no longer have the energy to continue doing so, you should bring your meditation session to a close. Even if you are in the middle of a *mālā*, you should stop and resume at some other time. To continue doing *japa* when you can no longer keep your mind focused is harmful to your practice. It can create a bad habit and predispose your mind to wander even more during future sessions.

Unfortunately, some meditators have already fallen into the habit of letting their minds wander during *japa*. Like most habits, this one is hard to break. Since it is associated with a particular mantra, this habit can be broken by setting that mantra aside and temporarily using another mantra. Then, by being extremely vigilant while using the new mantra, bringing the mind back immediately when it begins to wander, the habit can be broken over a period of weeks or months. Once it has been broken, use of the prior mantra can then be resumed.

Informal *Japa*

You can recite a mantra whenever you are unoccupied, wherever you happen to be: in your car while stuck in traffic, at work during a short break, in the supermarket while waiting in line, and so on. Even though you cannot actually meditate in such situations, reciting a mantra still helps focus and quiet your mind. And since mantras are prayers, this practice can bless you by turning your mind towards Ishvara at various times throughout the day.

An ideal occasion for informal *japa* is while walking. To recite a mantra while walking around the block or through a beautiful park is a delightful practice. It can be made even more compelling if you synchronize the mantra with your footsteps. With each step, you can recite one or more syllables of a mantra. Using your footsteps in this way is similar to using a *japa mālā*.

Any mantra can be synchronized with your gait. Some examples are given below, showing which syllable is to be recited with your right step (R) and with your left (L).

R   L   R L
om na – mah shi – vā – ya

R   L   R   L
om na – mo nā – rā – ya – nā – ya

R   L R   L R   L R L
om na – mo bha – ga – va – te vā – su – de – vā – ya

R L R   L   R L   R   L
om gam ga – na – pa – ta – ye na – ma - ha (silence)

R   L   R   L   R   L   R   L
om shrī rām jay rām jay jay rām

The meanings of these mantras can be found in Appendix A.

For mantras not listed above, you can experiment and invent your own patterns. It is desirable to use an even number of steps so that you always begin the mantra with your right foot.

You might need to practice a bit to get the hang of this technique. It becomes effortless after a while. Then you can enjoy reciting your mantra rhythmically along with your footsteps. If you find this practice difficult or awkward, you can simply recite the mantra silently while walking, disregarding your footsteps completely.

Exercise 4-4

Walking *Japa*

Preparation:

Go to a pleasant place suitable for walking. Make a *sankalpa* to set aside your problems and concerns as in Exercise 1-1. If you are accompanied by someone, agree to remain silent for the duration of the walk.

Practice:

Silently recite your mantra in synchronization with your footsteps. Walk at a natural, comfortable pace, beginning each mantra with your right foot. When your mind wanders, gently bring it back to the mantra.

Options:

If you find it difficult or awkward to synchronize your mantra to your footsteps, simply recite the mantra silently while walking, ignoring your footsteps.

CHAPTER FIVE

WITNESSING YOUR MIND

The prior chapters have explored forms of meditation in which your attention is focused or concentrated upon a particular object of meditation. Concentration, as explained in the introduction, is one of the four basic categories of meditation discussed in this book. Once again, the categories are: 1) concentration, 2) observation, 3) contemplation, and 4) devotion.

In this chapter, we will proceed to the second of the four categories, observation. The following definition was given in the introduction:

> Observation — watching the activities of your mind
> without being engaged in the process of thinking;
> being a detached witness to all mental activities.

This approach to meditation is completely different from all that has been discussed so far. In the preceding chapters, the importance of controlling your mind and focusing your attention was emphasized. Now we will discuss forms of meditation in which you *observe* your mental activities instead of trying to *control* them.

The concept of observing your thoughts may seem strange at first. After all, you are the thinker of your thoughts. But you are more than that. You have a mind; it belongs to you. So we can ask: To whom does your mind belong? Who is it that knows what your mind is thinking right now? Who directs its activities?

These thorny questions were contemplated by the ancient *rishis*. The profound inquiry of one such *rishi* is recorded in the Kena Upanishad. He began as follows:

केनेषितं पतति प्रेषितं मनः ।

keneshitam patati preshitam manah

Impelled by what does the mind think?

KeU 1.1

In the very next verse, he answers his own question by describing that which impels the mind as *"manasah manah* — the mind of the mind." With these words, he describes a reality that lies beyond our minds, something that endows our minds with the capacity for thinking. He thus began a fundamental spiritual inquiry, a quest that lies at the very heart of Vedantic teachings. That crucial investigation is, "Who am I?"

Knower and Known

Vedanta employs a simple but powerful mode of analysis to explore the question, "Who am I?" It begins by separating everything into two categories — knower and known. You, of course, are the knower. All else is known to you. The world is known to you. People are known to you. Houses and cars and trees are known to you. Even your own body is known to you.

In the Bhagavad Gita, Sri Krishna teaches Arjuna to differentiate the knower from the known. In the following verse, he refers to the known as the field of experience:

इदं शरीरं कौन्तेय क्षेत्रमित्यभिधीयते ।
एतद्यो वेत्ति तं प्राहुः क्षेत्रज्ञ इति तद्विदः ॥

idam shariram kaunteya kshetram ityabhidhiyate
etad yo vetti tam prahuh kshetrajna iti tad-vidah

O Arjuna, your body belongs to the field of experience.
The wise say: He who knows the body
is the knower of the field of experience.

BG 13.1

According to this passage, the simplest answer to the question, "Who am I?" is "I am the knower." Through its methodical teachings, Vedanta shows the knower's true nature to be pure consciousness, *sat cit ānanda*, the unborn, limitless true self, *ātmā*. These teachings require extensive explanation, much more than we can consider here. However, this subject will be briefly addressed in Chapter Nine which introduces advanced topics and techniques.

In the present chapter, let us confine our discussion to your day-to-day experience. You are the knower of all that you see, hear, taste, smell, and touch. You are the knower of your own body. You are also the knower of your thoughts and emotions. You know what you are thinking right now. You also know the presence or absence of happiness, sadness, hurt, and anger.

You are the knower of all your mental activities, all your *vrittis*. These *vrittis* include your thoughts, emotions, and perceptions. Each one of them is known to you; you are aware of them all. In Vedanta, the term *sākshī* or witness describes you as the awareful witness or conscious observer of your *vrittis*.

Sākshī Bhāva — Witnessing Your Mind

At this moment, your mind is engaged in reading this paragraph. Your attention is focused here on the book, not elsewhere. But you could shift your attention away from this book and focus instead on the activities of your mind. Then instead of reading this paragraph, you could observe your own thoughts, you could witness the *vrittis* of your mind. This condition is known as *sākshī bhāva*, the perspective or state (*bhāva*) of being a witness.

The term *sākshī bhāva* is used to describe the practice of observing the activities of your mind. In this practice, you witness your thoughts, emotions, and perceptions as they appear upon the landscape of your mind and then fade away. Instead of thinking your thoughts, you must detach yourself from your mind and observe the thoughts as if watching from a distance. From such a perspective, you can remain as a passive witness to the constantly changing flow of *vrittis* in your mind.

Patanjali notes that the observer of thoughts, *sākshī*, is completely unaffected by the thoughts observed. He explains this in the following *sutra*, using the word *drashtā* or seer instead of *sākshī*:

द्रष्टा दृशिमात्रः शुद्धोऽपि प्रत्ययानुपश्यतः ॥

drashtā drishi-mātrah shuddho 'pi pratyayānupashyatah

The seer, which is simply the capacity to observe, witnesses thoughts without being affected.

YS 2.20

To remain unaffected by mental activities during the practice of *sākshī bhāva*, you cannot be involved with what you observe. You cannot pass mental comments about thoughts or make judgments about your emotions. Each thought, perception, and emotion is neither desirable nor undesirable, neither good nor bad. Every *vritti* is simply a fact, just another mental event to be witnessed by you.

Sākshī bhāva is a useful and popular meditation technique. It is better known today in its Buddhist form—*vipassanā*, also known as mindfulness meditation. *Vipassanā* is a Pali word derived from the Sanskrit *vipashyanā* which means seeing clearly. For this reason, *vipassanā* is also called insight meditation. There are some differences between the Vedantic practice of *sākshī bhāva* and the Buddhist practice *vipassanā*. These differences may be of interest to scholars but are inconsequential for most meditators.

To practice *sākshī bhāva*, you must develop the skill of remaining as a detached observer, as a passive witness to your thoughts, emotions, and perceptions. This skill can be developed in stages. Because it is so easy to get entangled in thoughts and emotions, it is helpful at first to observe only your perceptions. By witnessing various sensations in your body, you can build the skills necessary for the practice of *sākshī bhāva*.

The following meditation exercise describes a method of observing physical sensations as they arise in each part of your body.

Exercise 5-1

Witnessing Body Sensations

Preparation:

Sit with proper posture, close your eyes, and make a *sankalpa* to set aside your concerns as in Exercise 1-1. Instead of the progressive relaxation exercise, simply take several deep breaths to settle your mind.

Practice – Part 1:

Turn your attention to each area of your body listed below, one at a time. Become aware of any physical sensations there, including the feeling of weight, pressure, warmth, coolness, and the touch of your clothing. Give the sensations your full attention. Observe them closely and make no mental comments about them. If no particular sensations are found, then observe the absence of sensations. Take about a minute to witness each area before shifting your attention to the next.

1. Feet, ankles, calves
2. Knees, thighs
3. Trunk, lower back, stomach
4. Upper back, chest, shoulders
5. Right arm, hand, fingers
6. Left arm, hand, fingers
7. Neck, head, face

Practice – Part 2:

Observe sensations arising anywhere in your body. Give the sensations your full attention. Observe them closely and make no mental comments about them. Continue for ten minutes or more.

Options:

If you have difficulty with the above practice, try naming or labeling each sensation as you observe it. For example, when you observe the weight of your hands resting in your lap, label it mentally, "Weight, weight." If you feel an itch on your nose, label it, "Itch, itch."

In the next meditation exercise, instead of observing sensations in your body, you will observe sensations associated with your breathing. This will help develop your ability to remain as a detached observer.

Exercise 5-2

Witnessing Your Breath

Preparation:

Sit with proper posture, close your eyes, and make a *sankalpa* to set aside your concerns as in Exercise 1-1. Instead of the progressive relaxation exercise, simply take several deep breaths to settle your mind.

Practice – Part 1:

Following the steps in the first part of Exercise 5-1 above, observe sensations in each part of your body. Take at least several minutes to scan your body from feet to head.

Practice – Part 2:

Observe your breath using the *prāna vīkshana* technique described in Exercise 1-2. Trace the passage of air with each breath. As you inhale, observe the air entering your nostrils, traveling down your windpipe, and filling your lungs. As you exhale, observe the air gradually being released from your lungs, traveling up your windpipe, and leaving your nostrils. Continue for five minutes or more.

Practice – Part 3:

Shift your attention to your nose and become aware of the subtle sensations inside your nostrils as air enters and leaves. As you inhale, notice that the air feels cool and dry. As you exhale, notice that the air from your lungs feels warm and moist. Try to notice the sensation on your upper lip as air blows across it during exhalation. Continue for five minutes or more.

Practice – Part 4:

Observe sensations in your entire body with each inhalation and exhalation. As you do so, reflect on the following: It takes no effort to breathe. Breathing is automatic, spontaneous, and effortless. In fact, you really don't breathe; it is your body that breathes. You just watch passively as your body breathes.

Imagine your body to be like a breathing statue as you observe it inhale and exhale repeatedly. Continue for five minutes or more.

Options:

Regarding the practice of Parts 2-4, if a part is entirely ineffective for you, it may be skipped. On the other hand, if you find one part to be particularly effective, you may extend its length as long as you like.

Exploring Your Mind

The two practices just described—observing physical sensations and observing your breathing—are both useful meditation techniques on their own. They also prepare you for *sākshī bhāva*, the practice of observing all mental events. All your thoughts, emotions, and perceptions occur in your mind, not elsewhere. Emotions may cause tightness or warmth in your chest, but they actually arise in your mind. Perception occurs when your mind receives images, sounds, smells, tastes, and touch from your sense organs. Thus every thought, emotion, and perception you experience exists in your mind as a *vritti*, a mental event.

In the practice of *sākshī bhāva*, all these *vritti*s are to be observed with detachment, as though from a distance. A helpful metaphor is to think of your mind as a room full of objects, the objects being your thoughts, emotions, and perceptions. The room of your mind is usually cluttered with an amazing jumble of articles. Much of that jumble is due to your thoughts—ideas, opinions, planning, problem solving, and so on. Because your thoughts are constantly changing, they continually fade from the room of your mind as new ones appear.

Among the articles in the room of your mind are various emotions, like the frustration of being stuck in a traffic jam, the hurt from someone's harsh words, or the joy due to a promotion or birth of a child. Like your thoughts, your emotions also change constantly, but they change more slowly than your fleeting thoughts. A particular emotion might fade from the room of your mind over a period of minutes or hours, though new emotions can emerge much more rapidly.

Your overall mood is unlike particular emotions. Mood changes more slowly than emotions and is less connected to specific events. Mood is like the quality of light in the room of your mind—sometimes dark and dreary, sometimes bright and cheerful, slowly shifting from one ambiance to another over a period of hours or days.

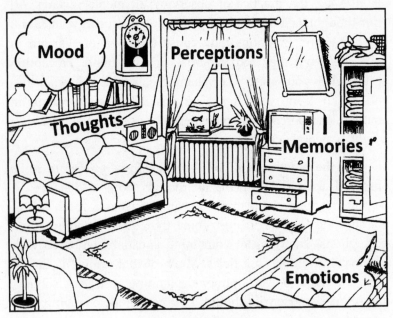

Room of Your Mind

Perceptions enter the room of your mind through the windows of your senses. These five windows look out on the world and allow a diverse assortment of sights, sounds, smells, tastes, and touch to shine in. At night when you sleep, blinds are drawn over these windows, preventing sensations from entering. But all day long, the room of your mind is constantly flooded by an ever-changing assortment of sensations.

The room of your mind is furnished with cabinets, chests and closets — ample storage for all your memories. When you choose to, you can open the door to a closet of memories and retrieve items from the past. Sometimes, an overflowing accumulation of memories can push the door open, allowing memories to haphazardly spill out into the room of your mind. Whether memories are intentionally retrieved or if they tumble out of a closet, the result is the same: they fill the room of your mind with more *vrittis*.

Memories are not merely factual accounts of past events; they include emotions and perceptions associated with the events. For example, when you recall a joyous celebration, happy feelings arise along with the sights and sounds of the occasion. And when you recall the loss of a loved one, sadness arises together with vivid images of major events. Thus memories fill the room of your mind with even more thoughts, emotions, and perceptions.

Being a Detached Observer

In the practice of *sakshī bhāva*, it is essential to remain completely detached from everything you observe in the room of your mind. The Bhagavad Gita describes this detachment in the following verse:

उदासीनवदासीनो गुणैर्यो न विचाल्यते ।
गुणा वर्तन्त इत्येव योऽवतिष्ठति नेङ्गते ॥

udāsīnavad āsīno gunair yo na vicālyate
gunā vartanta ityeva yo 'vatishthati nengate

One who sits like a detached onlooker
is not affected by the *guna*s (qualities).
Knowing that *guna*s act on their own, he remains undisturbed.

BG 14.23

*Guna*s are the basic qualities of nature—the principles of
purity (*sattva*), activity (*rajas*), and inertia (*tamas*). In the verse
above, *guna*s refer to the qualities of your mind, more
specifically, the nature of your *vritti*s. With this in mind, the
verse could be paraphrased as follows:

One who sits like a detached onlooker
is not affected by the *vritti*s of one's mind.
Knowing that *vritti*s act on their own, he remains undisturbed.

To completely disentangle yourself from your mind's
activities, some kind of distance or separation between you and
your mind is required. You cannot be a detached observer as
long as you remain in the room of your mind, thinking your
thoughts, feeling your emotions, and perceiving your
sensations. Instead of thinking your thoughts, you must watch
them. Instead of feeling your emotions, you must observe
them. And instead of perceiving your sensations, you must
witness them.

Sākshī bhāva requires a radical shift of perspective—a
view from outside the room of your mind. You must
figuratively leave the room of your mind and observe its
contents from outside. This shift is depicted by the following
illustrations.

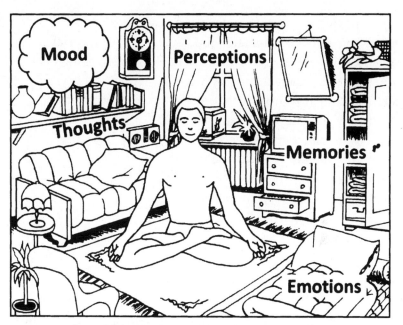

Before *Sākshī Bhāva*—Inside the Room of Your Mind

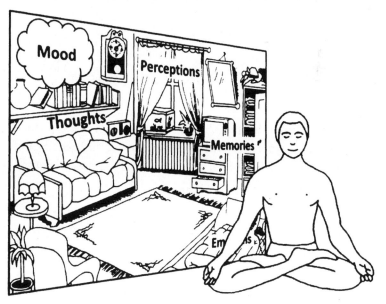

During *Sākshī Bhāva*—Observing Your Mind From Outside

To shift your point of view and observe the room of your mind from outside is a matter of perspective; it simply depends on how you look at your mind. In the illustration shown here, you can see either a vase or two faces looking towards each other. With some practice, you can easily shift from one perspective to the other. In the same way, you can learn to shift your perspective from inside the room of your mind to outside. You can make this shift by simply choosing to witness each of your thoughts, emotions, and perceptions instead of thinking, feeling, and seeing them.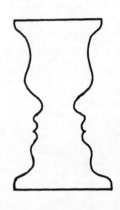

The following meditation exercise provides detailed instructions for the practice of *sākshī bhāva*.

Exercise 5-3

Sākshī Bhāva – Witnessing Your Mind

Preparation:

Sit with proper posture, close your eyes, and make a *sankalpa* to set aside your concerns as in Exercise 1-1. Instead of the progressive relaxation exercise, simply take several deep breaths to settle your mind.

Practice – Part 1:

Following the steps in the first part of Exercise 5-1, observe sensations in each part of your body. Take at least five minutes to scan your body from feet to head.

Practice – Part 2:

Following the steps in Exercise 5-2, observe your breathing. Begin by tracing the passage of air with each breath. Then observe sensations at your nostrils. Finally, observe sensations in your entire body as it breathes automatically like a breathing statue. Take at least five minutes to complete these steps.

Practice – Part 3:

Shift your perspective to detach and separate yourself from your mind so that you can observe its activities as though from a distance. Imagine yourself sitting outside the room of your mind, looking within and observing its contents.

Witness any thoughts passing through the room of your mind, keeping them at a distance. Observe any emotions that happen to be present, without letting them affect you. Notice the emotional brightness or darkness of the room. Witness any sensations entering through your five windows of perception.

Make no judgments or mental comments about anything observed. Each *vritti* is merely a factual event to be witnessed passively. Continue for ten minutes or more.

Options:

If you have difficulty with Part 3, try labeling or naming each thought, emotion, and perception as it arises. For example, if frustration arises, mentally label it, "Emotion, emotion." If you feel an ache in your knee, label it, "Perception, perception." And for each thought that arises, label it, "Thought, thought."

The Practice of Mindfulness

After practicing the meditation exercises in this chapter over a period of time, your ability to witness mental activities without getting entangled in them will grow stronger. As that skill develops, you might occasionally find yourself observing your mind while you are busily engaged in daily tasks. As mentioned in the previous chapter, your mind is well equipped for multitasking. You can clean your kitchen or drive your car while simultaneously witnessing your *vrittis*. It is not difficult to keep a small fraction of your attention separate from your activities for the sake of self-observation.

To observe ourselves while engaged in daily activities is called the practice of mindfulness. It can be an exceptionally transformative spiritual practice because of its ability to reveal hidden facets of our minds. According to the teachings of Vedanta, suffering is the result of ignorance about ourselves. This self-ignorance is partly psychological and partly fundamental. Fundamentally, we fail to know our true selves as *sat cit ānanda*, as pure consciousness—unborn, eternal, perfect, and limitless. Psychologically, we fail to fully understand the complicated workings of our own minds.

Vedantic teachings are meant to remove ignorance about *ātmā*, the true self. But they do not directly address our psychological blind spots like unhealed emotional wounds and repressed anger. In fact, the teachings of Vedanta assume we have already dealt with such issues before embarking on the quest for spiritual wisdom. Buried psychological problems must be resolved to gain the degree of emotional maturity required for serious Vedantic inquiry. To resolve such problems, we must first understand the way our minds work; we must understand ourselves psychologically.

We can learn so much by simply observing our thoughts, emotions, and behavior throughout the day. But we seldom find opportunities to be introspective when we are busily engaged in our daily affairs. And in the absence of such introspection, important insights about ourselves can remain hidden like valuable books stuffed in the corner of a closet.

With some effort, a highly beneficial habit of self-observation can be cultivated. This practice of mindfulness can reveal important insights about the inner forces that motivate our actions. Such insights can help us make better decisions and shape our futures more skillfully. This fact is beautifully expressed in a much-quoted anonymous saying:

Watch your thoughts, for they become words.
Watch your words, for they become actions.
Watch your actions, for they become habits.
Watch your habits, for they become character.
Watch your character, for it becomes your destiny.

It is possible to trace your actions back to the thoughts from which they arose by simply asking yourself, "Why did I do that?" In time, you can take a further step and trace those decisive thoughts back to the subconscious impulses and desires from which they arose. The practice of *sākshī bhāva* can prepare you for this kind of inquiry.

125

When we dive deep into our psyches to discover the mysterious impulses from which our thoughts emerge, we may stumble upon aspects of ourselves that are unpleasant and unwanted. Jealousy, hurt, anger, and pride lurk in the minds of us all. Such issues must be handled appropriately, in healthy, healing ways. These important topics will be explored in the next two chapters.

In the practice of mindfulness and self-observation, it is essential to avoid any kind of self-criticism or self-judgment. Every thought, desire, and impulse you discover through introspection is a fact to be understood, not a reason to criticize yourself. It is crucial that you remain detached and objective in this practice.

If self-observation leads you to make harsh judgments about yourself, it is best to set this practice aside for the time being. The next two chapters will address issues relating to self-judgment and self-criticism. After reading those chapters and performing the meditation exercises included, you can then return to this practice of mindfulness.

The following exercise provides suggestions for how you can cultivate the practice of mindfulness throughout the day.

Exercise 5-4

Mindfulness:
Observing Your Thoughts and Behavior

Tasks as Reminders:
Immediately before or after a task is a perfect time to pause for a few moments of self-reflection. After completing one task and before starting the next, stop briefly to observe your thoughts, emotions, and behavior.

Suitable occasions include:

> Before or after a phone call or conversation.
> Before or after sending an email or text message.
> Before a meal or after cleaning up.
> Before going to bed or after getting up.
> After turning off the television.
> After starting your car or parking it.

Choose one or more of the above as reminders to pause for self-observation.

Waiting:

> Any time you spend waiting is ideal for the practice of mindfulness. You can reflect on your thoughts, emotions, and behavior while:

> > Waiting at a stop light or in heavy traffic.
> > Waiting in line or riding an elevator.
> > Waiting for someone to arrive.

Periodic Reflection:

> At the beginning of each hour throughout the day, take a one-minute break to reflect on your thoughts, emotions, and behavior. Alternatively, take a half-minute break every quarter hour.

Mindful Activity:

> Some activities which are not particularly demanding are especially well suited for the practice of mindfulness. Hold a small part of your attention separate so that you can observe your thoughts, emotions, and behavior while engaged in that activity. Suitable occasions for this practice include:

> > Going for a walk.
> > Eating a meal.
> > Driving your car (drive safely!)
> > Cleaning your house, room, desk, etc.

CHAPTER SIX

THE PSYCHOLOGY OF MEDITATION

You have probably noticed how memories, worries, and even fears can sometimes arise when you meditate. Those memories might include unpleasant recollections of painful events and past difficulties. Such memories, worries, and fears can emerge abruptly, for no apparent reason, even in the midst of deep meditation. Experiences like these may seem mystifying, but they are the result of hidden, unconscious forces that can be clearly identified. To understand these hidden forces, we must explore the psychology of meditation.

The discoveries of Sigmund Freud, Carl Jung, and other eminent researchers have shown that every person possesses both a conscious mind and an unconscious mind. Your conscious mind is composed of thoughts, emotions, and perceptions; all these *vritti*s are experienced by you. Your unconscious mind, on the other hand, has a completely different makeup and it remains hidden, outside your experience.

Unconscious aspects of our minds are also recognized and explained by the teachings of Vedanta. This chapter is based both on Vedanta and modern psychology, although the term unconscious is used somewhat differently here than how Freud used it.

Your unconscious mind is a vast repository of memories, fears, desires, and other things that can emerge into your conscious mind as thoughts and emotions. Your unconscious mind is a complicated assemblage of elements. These elements include *vāsanas* which Vedanta describes as deep-seated desires and hidden impulses. Vedanta also describes the presence of *samskāras* — mental impressions or conditioning which remain from past experiences or past lives. Modern psychology has identified other aspects of the unconscious, including the *id* which is the source of powerful basic instincts, including sexual drives. Psychology also recognizes the presence of the *superego* or conscience — your innate sense of right and wrong.

To thoroughly explore these complex and enigmatic features of the unconscious is well beyond the scope of this book. However, the brief description above is sufficient to reveal powerful unseen forces and a vast store of memories, all of which are hidden from your conscious mind. From this hidden source, memories, fears, desires, and other things can emerge while you meditate.

Unconscious matter seems to emerge more freely during meditation than at other times. Such is the mind's nature. When your mind is active, the presence of numerous *vrittis* inhibits the emergence of matter from your unconscious. But when your mind is quieted by meditation, fewer *vrittis* are present to push that stuff away, allowing memories, fears, and desires to emerge from your unconscious more freely. According to the maxim, "Nature abhors a vacuum," a quiet mind is an ideal space into which matter from the unconscious can emerge.

To help explain this phenomenon, a bottle of carbonated soda provides a surprisingly apt analogy. Invisible carbon dioxide gas is dissolved in soda like memories, fears, and desires are hidden in your unconscious. You cannot see the dissolved gas in the soda, nor can you directly experience the matter residing in your unconscious. When the bottle is opened, dissolved gas starts to bubble up from the soda. Likewise when you meditate, memories, fears, and desires start to emerge into your conscious mind, metaphorically bubbling up from your unconscious. Let us examine why this happens.

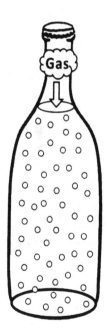

What is it that keeps the carbonation dissolved in soda and prevents it from bubbling up? You may have noticed that bottles are never completely filled; there is always an empty space at the top. That space is actually filled with pressurized gas. Its pressure pushes down on the soda and keeps the dissolved gas from escaping. When the cap is removed from the bottle, the pressure is released and dissolved gas can then bubble up from the soda.

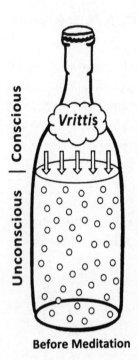

Before Meditation

Applying this analogy, your conscious mind is usually filled with thoughts, emotions, and perceptions. All these *vrittis* exert pressure on your unconscious mind. This inhibits memories, fears, and desires from emerging just like pressure at the top of a bottle prevents dissolved gas from bubbling up. As long as the bottle is tightly capped, pressure is maintained and bubbles cannot emerge. Similarly, as long as your conscious mind is filled with *vrittis*, mental pressure is maintained and unconscious matter is prevented from bubbling up into consciousness.

Meditation has the opposite effect; it is like opening the bottle. When the cap is removed, pressure is released which allows bubbles to emerge. In the same way, when your mind is quieted by meditation, there are few *vrittis* left to exert pressure on your unconscious mind. And in the absence of that pressure, memories, fears, and desires can bubble up into your conscious mind just like a fizzing bottle of soda.

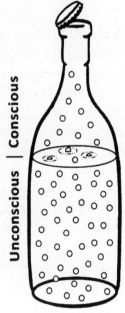

During Meditation

The next question is, "Why do particular memories, fears, and desires arise and not others?" Unconscious matter seems to emerge according to its intensity. For example, memories of painful or traumatic events are more likely to emerge than those of everyday affairs. Angry arguments, stinging hurts, and infuriating conflicts can create memories possessing enormous energy. With such power, they can force themselves into your conscious mind. Amazingly, some painful memories retain their intense power even if the events occurred many years ago. The tremendous force exerted by such memories is an issue that meditators cannot ignore.

Pressure of the Unconscious Mind

Returning to our soda bottle analogy, the gas dissolved in soda exerts pressure to escape as bubbles. Highly carbonated soda exerts more pressure than less carbonated soda. And if the soda is warm or shaken, even more pressure will be exerted by the gas. These facts can help explain the often mysterious behavior of the forces hidden in your unconscious mind.

The pressure exerted by dissolved gas represents the pressure exerted by memories, fears, and desires to emerge into your conscious mind. Just as greater carbonation creates more pressure, so too, unconscious matter of greater intensity exerts more pressure. And just like a warm bottle of soda can erupt with a stream of foam when shaken, matter from the unconscious can likewise erupt with great force when you get emotionally heated or agitated. Not surprisingly, we say that people sometimes blow up like a volcano—a vivid and fitting analogy indeed.

The Shvetashvatara Upanishad provides a different metaphor to describe the nature of an agitated mind:

दुष्टाश्वयुक्तमिव वाहमेनं ।

dushtāshva-yuktam iva vāham enam

This (mind) is like a chariot yoked to wild horses.   ShvU 2.9

Memories, fears, and desires can emerge into your conscious mind at any time, not just during meditation. For example, traumatic memories can erupt while at home, work, or elsewhere and suddenly plunge one into emotional turmoil. Therapists and self-help books offer extensive advice on how to manage such problems. In this chapter, however, we will focus on ways in which meditation can help manage smaller, more typical issues that meditators are likely to face.

Every day, you experience many little irritations, hurts, frustrations, and disappointments. Each of these leave a trace or remnant in your unconscious. If the remnants accumulate over a period of time, the pressure they exert can gradually build up. And if the pressure grows large enough, the accumulation can forcefully erupt, leading you to lose your temper or suffer a so-called emotional meltdown. Everyone is subject to such outbursts when inner pressures are allowed to build up.

To release pressure, you need time for your mind to quiet down so that accumulated unconscious matter can bubble up and be vented. Usually, leisure time gives you the opportunity to relax and let off steam. But sometimes, excessive demands prevent this. If a busy lifestyle continually prevents you from letting off steam, pressure can build up in your unconscious like a warm, shaken-up bottle of soda.

If you release a little bit of pressure each day, a dramatic explosion of pent-up pressure can be avoided. Daily meditation is an ideal way to vent that pressure. Meditation can quiet your mind enough to allow memories and other unconscious matter to bubble up and be released. In this way, meditation can play a therapeutic role. Meditation can help just like a relaxing vacation; it can provide a brief escape from your troubles and an opportunity to refresh yourself. Meditation can be a mini-holiday, a twenty or thirty minute vacation you can enjoy every day of the week.

The use of meditation to release built-up pressure is described in the following exercise.

Exercise 6-1

Releasing Inner Pressure

Preparation:

Sit with proper posture, close your eyes, and perform the progressive relaxation exercise as in Exercise 1-1. For this meditation, skip the step of making a *sankalpa*.

Practice – Part 1:

Begin by practicing any meditation technique from the prior chapters that you have found particularly effective in quieting your mind. Recommended practices include *Prāna Vīkshana* (Exercise 1-2), Slow Deep Breathing and *Ujjayī Prānāyāma* (Exercises 2-3 and 2-4), and Silent Mantra *Japa* (Exercise 4-2).

Practice – Part 2:

As your mind quiets down, memories and other matter may begin to bubble up from your unconscious. When this occurs, observe the emerging *vritti*s using the techniques of *Sākshī Bhāva* (Exercise 5-3). Remain as a detached witness. Shift your perspective to separate yourself from your *vritti*s, observing them as though from a distance. Make no judgments or mental comments about anything witnessed.

When the *vritti*s you are observing fade away, resume practicing the technique used in Part 1. When other *vritti*s bubble up, repeat this process, observing them as a passive witness and returning to the technique of Part 1 when they again fade away. Continue for ten minutes or more.

Conclusion:

After meditating, reflect on the particular thoughts and emotions that emerged from your unconscious. They might indicate unresolved issues in your life that require attention.

Coping with External Pressures

During meditation, the very same thought or memory can bubble up from your unconscious again and again. If the same thing keeps emerging, it is probably driven by a force that exerts great pressure. The source of this pressure could be a big problem or distressing predicament in your life that remains unresolved. Since numerous periods of difficulty and stress are inevitable in everyone's life, such experiences are not uncommon.

Meditation can reduce the stress and anxiety that accompany difficult situations. But meditation is no substitute for addressing the issues underlying those situations. As mentioned in the introduction, meditation is not a way to escape life's problems. To elaborate on this important point, I would like to share an anecdote that shows how I learned a sobering lesson about using meditation as an escape.

I once lived in my guru's ashram along with sixty other students undergoing a three-year residential course in Vedanta and Sanskrit. There was a great deal of camaraderie among us as we lived, worked, and studied together. Yet conflicts would inevitably arise now and again. On one occasion, I got into a big argument with a fellow student and exchanged harsh words with him. Later, I returned to my room feeling overcome by anger, hurt, and frustration.

My meditation practice had grown quite strong, so I chose to use it to free myself from the horrible feelings that burned inside me. I sat and began to recite my mantra. At first, painful memories of the argument bubbled up almost continuously, but I used my mantra to push them away. Eventually, these memories emerged less often. After much time and effort, I finally felt free from all the anger, hurt, and frustration that arose due to the argument.

Because those memories were so painful, it took a long time to push them away. I meditated for almost three hours then, much longer than my usual sessions. But I finally arose from my cushion feeling refreshed and relieved. Shortly after leaving my room, I happened to come across the student with whom I had argued. Even though we said nothing to each other, my feelings of anger, hurt, and frustration returned instantly with the same burning intensity I felt before. In that moment, the results of three hours of meditation were totally wiped out.

Meditation did nothing to resolve my conflict with the other student. It merely provided a short-lived escape by temporarily blocking my painful feelings. Returning to the soda bottle analogy, using meditation as an escape is like chilling the soda. When soda is cold, the gas dissolved in it exerts less pressure. But as soon as it warms up, the pressure returns. In the same way, meditation helped me to cool off – to chill, so to speak. But after my meditation session came to an end, the pressure within me soon returned to its full force.

To use meditation to escape from problems is both un-wise and a waste of time. On the other hand, meditation can be extremely useful in helping us cope with life's challenges by empowering us to respond to them more effectively. If we react frantically and impulsively to difficult situations, we can make things worse. But if we respond calmly and deliberately, our problems can be resolved more easily. Daily meditation can infuse us with an abiding sense of peace, centeredness, and detachment which can help us remain clear and composed even in the midst of a major crisis.

Meditation can also help us discover solutions to com-plex problems. Sometimes, we are like a person trapped in a room, furiously struggling to break open a locked door. If that person is totally focused on opening the door, his feverish efforts could actually prevent him from discovering an unlocked window and escaping through it. He would be wise to pause for a few moments and consider other solutions to his dilemma.

When addressing complicated situations, it is easy to jump to hasty conclusions about what needs to be done. But such conclusions can lead you to overlook other approaches that might be more effective. For this reason, it can be beneficial to step away from a problem for a while and ponder it calmly. Meditation is well suited for such reflection. In the stillness of meditation, any prior assumptions and conclusions about a problem can be set aside temporarily. When your mind has been opened in this way, you can more freely consider a wide range of possible solutions.

Meditation can give you a completely new perspective on a complex situation. If you feel lost and confused as if in a maze, meditation can figuratively lift you out of the maze so that you can see it from above. Meditation helps you see the big picture so you can find the best course of action. Even in the midst of a crisis, it can be enormously helpful to stop and reflect. To twist a common expression, "Don't just do something, sit there!"

The following exercise shows how meditation can be used to seek solutions for complicated problems.

Exercise 6-2

Meditation for Resolving Problems

Preparation:

Sit with proper posture, close your eyes, and perform the progressive relaxation exercise as in Exercise 1-1. For this meditation, skip the step of making a *sankalpa*.

Practice – Part 1:

Begin by practicing any meditation technique from the prior chapters that you have found particularly effective in quieting your mind. Recommended practices include *Prāna Vīkshana* (Exercise 1-2), Slow Deep Breathing and *Ujjayī Prānāyāma* (Exercises 2-3 and 2-4), and Silent Mantra *Japa* (Exercise 4-2). Continue for ten minutes or more.

Practice – Part 2:

After the above practice, allow the problem you wish to address to arise in your mind. Observe your thoughts about the problem using the techniques of *Sākshī Bhāva* (Exercise 5-3). Remain as a detached witness. Shift your perspective to separate yourself from your *vrittis*, observing them as though from a distance. Make no judgments or mental comments about anything witnessed.

Practice – Part 3:

After practicing *sākshī bhāva* for some time, allow yourself to actively ponder the problem. Explore as many approaches as possible, even if they seem unfeasible. If your mind returns to a previously considered solution, gently turn your attention away from it and let your innate creativity lead you to other possible solutions.

Dealing with Hurt and Resentment

Of all memories, those exerting the most pressure to emerge seem to be associated with hurt, resentment, bitterness, and so on. In my years of teaching, I have met so many people who have admitted to struggling with hurt and resentment that has lingered on from past events. Their painful feelings have often persisted for months, years, or even decades after the events. Such memories can arise unexpectedly and disrupt meditation sessions or trigger emotional turmoil. For these reasons, this section is dedicated specifically to handling issues regarding hurt and resentment.

You have probably noticed that some memories of distressing events no longer affect you while others seem to retain their sting—even now you wince each time they arise. Why are those particular memories still so painful, even if the events are long past? The short answer to this complex question is that your process of emotional healing is not yet complete. Only when you have let go of resentment and no longer blame anyone for your pain will that process be complete. Healing requires forgiveness of those who hurt you. Until they are forgiven, painful memories can continue to torment you.

Some might object and say, "But they do not deserve forgiveness! What they did was wrong; it was despicable, unforgivable. They hurt *me*. Why should I forgive *them*?" Such feelings are understandable. However, forgiveness is actually meant to help you, not them. Regardless of whether *they* deserve forgiveness or not, *you* deserve to be free from further suffering due to painful memories. Forgiveness is for your sake—it frees you from the past and removes the sting of unpleasant memories.

Many self-help books blithely assert, "You *must* forgive all those who have hurt you." Unfortunately, such books often fail to tell you *how* to forgive them. Forgiveness is not an act of will. Merely deciding to forgive someone does not remove your hurt, blame, and resentment. According to the teachings of Vedanta, ignorance is the underlying cause for all forms of suffering, including emotional hurt and resentment. In fact, ignorance is the main obstacle to forgiveness. Forgiveness requires a completely new perspective on the events that transpired. Forgiveness requires spiritual wisdom.

My guru often uses the following illustration: Suppose you were holding a two-year-old girl in your arms, taking care of the toddler. If she gets upset and begins swinging her arms around wildly, she could clobber your face hard enough to inflict considerable pain. Then, would you get angry at her and shout in rage? Or would your feelings be hurt because she hit you even though you were caring for her? Oddly enough, you would not feel even a trace of anger or emotional hurt. On the other hand, if an acquaintance slapped your face, you might become inflamed with anger and indignation. Or you might feel deeply wounded and sink into a pit of hurt, despair, and self-pity.

You would react differently to the toddler because you understand that she is incapable of controlling her behavior. She has not grown sufficiently mature to restrain her emotional and physical outbursts. But then, many adults also lack sufficient maturity to restrain their emotional and physical outbursts. When adults utter hurtful words or inflict harm on others, it is usually the result of their own uncontrolled emotional reactions. If they had grown sufficiently wise and self-disciplined, they would probably not behave in such ways. It is an undeniable fact that adults sometimes lose self-control. While toddlers have yet to develop self-control, adults can lose control temporarily, usually at times of great stress.

None of us are perfect. When we are overwhelmed by distress and turbulent emotions, it is all too easy to momentarily lose self-control and swerve from the path of dharma. And in those moments, we can harm someone just like a toddler who lacks self-control. *Prakriti,* the force of nature within us all, is so powerful that under certain circumstances we can find ourselves helplessly out of control. The Bhagavad Gita poignantly affirms this truth:

प्रकृतिं यान्ति भूतानि निग्रहः किं करिष्यति ।

prakritim yānti bhūtāni nigrahah kim karishyati

All creatures act according to nature.
What is the use of sheer restraint?

BG 3.33

Those who hurt you did so because they were overcome by the forces of *prakriti.* Those forces grew strong enough to drag them from the path of dharma and lead them to commit harmful, *adharmic* acts. As you come to understand and accept their helplessness and the inevitability of such acts, you will realize there is no reason to blame them or feel resentful. And when no trace of blame or resentment remains, you will find that forgiveness has already taken place in your heart. Your process of emotional healing will then be complete and painful memories of the hurtful event will no longer trouble you.

None of this is meant to suggest that hurtful behavior is somehow acceptable or that it should be tolerated. There is no excuse for acts of *adharma* and no justification for allowing others to hurt us. In fact, the principles of dharma dictate that we must always take appropriate steps to protect ourselves from harm. The discussion above encourages us to seek understanding and forgiveness, not complacency or passivity.

The following meditation exercise can help you let go of any blame or resentment lingering from past events. It is based on the third of the four basic categories of techniques— contemplation. Contemplation uses specific kinds of thought and reflection to change our patterns of thinking. This category of meditation will be thoroughly explored in the next chapter.

Before undertaking the practice below, you will need to select two specific events from your life to reflect upon:

1. An incident in which someone hurt you and you continue to blame the person and feel resentful.

2. A similar incident in which you hurt someone else.

Exercise 6-3

Meditation for Forgiveness

Preparation:
Following the steps in Exercise 1-1, sit with proper posture, close your eyes, make a *sankalpa* to set aside your concerns, and perform the progressive relaxation exercise.

Practice – Part 1:

Begin by practicing any meditation technique from the prior chapters that you have found particularly effective in quieting your mind. Recommended practices include *Prāna Vīkshana* (Exercise 1-2), Slow Deep Breathing and *Ujjayī Prānāyāma* (Exercises 2-3 and 2-4), and Silent Mantra *Japa* (Exercise 4-2). Continue for ten minutes or more.

Practice – Part 2:

Stop practicing the above technique and recall the incident in which you hurt someone. Visualize the person you hurt and the setting of the event. Recall what transpired with as much detail as possible. Reflect on the harm and suffering your behavior inflicted on the person.

Next, reflect on the inner forces of *prakriti* that led you to behave in that manner. Recall the particular circumstances and intense emotions that may have overwhelmed you and led you to lose self-control. Recognize your own helplessness at that moment. Finally, forgive yourself for your harmful behavior and pray for forgiveness from the person you hurt.

Practice – Part 3:

Recall the incident in which someone hurt you. Visualize the person and the setting of the event. Recall what transpired with as much detail as possible. Reflect on the harm and pain you suffered due to the person's behavior.

Next, reflect on the inner forces of *prakriti* that may have led that person to behave in a harmful manner. Try to understand the particular circumstances and intense emotions that may have overwhelmed the person, leading to loss of self-control. Recognize the person's helplessness at that moment. Finally, let go of any blame or resentment you have held on to and prayerfully offer your forgiveness to the person.

Coping with Loss — Letting Go

There are times when our hearts are filled with pain and hurt, yet there is no one to forgive and nothing that can be done. We suffer when loved ones die. We suffer when children grow up and move away, leaving homes empty. We suffer when the vitality and enthusiasm of our early years gives way to responsibilities and routines in middle age, and eventually culminates in the inexorable decline of health with old age.

Losses like these are inevitable. We know this intellectually, yet we still want to hold on to all we enjoy — family, security, lifestyle, health, and so on. We are reluctant or even unable to let go, even when uncontrollable circumstances snatch things away from us. Yet, if we constantly grasp at what is slipping away, our minds will churn with grief, worry, and regret. Whatever losses we must endure, grasping and regret will only magnify our suffering.

By resisting change and clinging to the past, we unwittingly ensnare ourselves in suffering like the monkey in the following account. In rural India, a clever monkey trap is fashioned from a coconut pierced with a hole just big enough for a monkey's hand to slip through. Food is placed in the coconut to lure a monkey to reach inside. When it grasps the food, its hand becomes too big to fit through the narrow hole. If

146

the monkey were to let go of the food, its hand could easily be withdrawn. But as long as the monkey holds on to the food, its hand cannot be extracted. The monkey is trapped by its own act of grasping.

When we grasp after things that are unavoidably slipping away with the passage of time, we trap ourselves in a net of grief, worry, and regret. When we try to stop the unstoppable or control the uncontrollable, we end up thrashing about wildly in that net and become even more entangled in its web. Ironically, we can free ourselves from that net of grief, worry, and regret if we simply stop grasping and thrashing about.

What can we do to let go? Vedantic teachings and specific meditation techniques can loosen our grip on the past and help us gracefully accept the inevitable losses of life. According to the teachings of Vedanta, all losses occur due to the laws of nature which are God's laws, Ishvara's laws, Ishvara's natural order. We can understand the laws of nature as expressions of Ishvara's will, as the will of Almighty God.

The laws of nature, including the law of karma, are a manifestation of Ishvara's intelligence, an expression of God's cosmic order. In the Bhagavad Gita, Sri Krishna says, "*kālo 'smi*, I am time."(11.32) In this verse, time represents all laws of nature. Thus Sri Krishna, speaking as Ishvara, declares that He is manifest in the world as the laws of nature. A few verses later, Arjuna responds by saying, "*sthāne hrishīkesha*, O Krishna, everything is as it must be."(11.36) Arjuna knew that terrible losses on the battlefield were inescapable. He learned to accept this horrific fact with the help of Sri Krishna's teachings.

To gracefully accept losses in life requires deep comprehension of Ishvara's will and thorough knowledge of the natural order of the world, including the laws of karma. These important topics cannot be thoroughly explored in this book, but they are completely unfolded in the Bhagavad Gita, especially in the second and third chapters. Those teachings can help us gain equanimity towards the inevitable losses of life. In chapter two, Sri Krishna says:

सिद्ध्यसिद्ध्योः समो भूत्वा समत्वं योग उच्यते ।

siddhy-asiddhyoh samo bhūtvā samatvam yoga ucyate

Treat success and failure alike. Yoga is equanimity.

BG 2.48

The very same wisdom about graceful acceptance is also expressed in the well-known Serenity Prayer:

God grant me serenity
to accept the things I cannot change,
courage to change the things I can,
and wisdom to know the difference.

Spiritual wisdom and certain meditation techniques can help us let go of unnecessary burdens we might bear from trying to change the unchangeable or restrain what cannot be stopped. We often hold ourselves responsible for situations over which we have no control. We want everyone to be happy and healthy at all times. We want every situation to be pleasant and peaceful. We try very hard to accomplish all this, yet we often encounter immovable obstacles.

For example, when a loved one lies dying in the hospital and doctors say nothing more can reasonably be done, family members sometimes request extreme measures be employed. Such measures might forestall death by a few hours or days, but they only delay the inevitable. They also drag family members into an agonizing, prolonged, and ultimately futile struggle. When family members assume responsibility for preventing death's inevitable approach, they take upon their shoulders burdens that are unreasonable and unbearable.

Imagine a heavily-laden raft floating down a shallow stream full of protruding rocks. The raft will surely get stuck on the rocks again and again. Conversely, imagine a small leaf floating down the same stream. Due to its lightness, the leaf can skim along the stream's surface, nimbly avoiding each obstacle. Its downstream journey will be speedy and effortless. This metaphor suggests that when we are heavily burdened with unreasonable concerns, we can get stuck in life. We can become paralyzed by our emotions and unable to move on. But if we unburden our hearts and let go of unreasonable concerns, then we can nimbly skirt around the obstacles of life and journey onwards like the leaf.

Several meditation techniques can help you let go of unreasonable and unnecessary burdens. Slow Deep Breathing (Exercise 2-3) is useful, especially if you recite the words peace and release during inhalation and exhalation. A powerful traditional technique is to practice *japa* of the Mahamrityunjaya Mantra. This mantra is specifically intended to be used at times of uncontrollable change and loss. It is included in Appendix A together with an explanation of its meaning.

The following meditation exercise describes another method for letting go of unreasonable burdens by using *ujjayī prāṇāyāma.*

Exercise 6-4

Ujjayī Prānāyāma for Letting Go

Preparation:

Following the steps in Exercise 1-1, sit with proper posture, close your eyes, make a *sankalpa* to set aside your concerns, and perform the progressive relaxation exercise.

Practice:

Begin to practice *ujjayī prānāyāma*, following the instructions in Exercise 2-4. Use yogic breathing to fill your lungs completely. Trace the passage of air with each breath. As you exhale, slightly constrict your larynx muscles to restrict the air flow and listen for the hissing sound.

With each exhalation, imagine yourself letting go of all your burdens. Use each exhalation as an opportunity to empty yourself, more and more completely, of any remaining heaviness of heart and mind. Feel your heart growing lighter with each exhalation. With each inhalation, imagine yourself being filled with peace, contentment, and well-being. Continue for ten minutes or more.

Options:

To deepen your practice, inhale a bit more deeply and exhale a bit more slowly, pausing for a second or two with your lungs full before each exhalation. Be careful to avoid causing any discomfort or strain.

Conclusion:

Allow your larynx muscles to relax and breathe normally. Observe how you feel for a few moments before slowly opening your eyes.

CHAPTER SEVEN

MEDITATION
FOR EMOTIONAL GROWTH

The prior chapter dealt with psychological and emotional issues to an extent not usually found in books like this based on Vedantic teachings. Indeed, the ancient *rishis* and revered teachers like Shankara never specifically mentioned unconscious mind, pent-up stress, or emotional healing. These topics are clearly of modern origin.

However, Shankara and the *rishis* did not ignore psychological and emotional issues. They directly addressed these topics, but they used different terminology than we do today. Instead of asserting the need for emotional healing and releasing stress, they set forth the need for inner purification, for purity of mind. They taught that *antahkarana shuddhi*, purity (*shuddhi*) of mind (*antahkarana*) is a vital requisite for spiritual growth.

Patanjali also asserts the need for inner purity. He refers to it as *citta prasāda* (*citta*–mind, *prasāda*–purity) in the following *sutra*:

मैत्रीकरुणामुदितोपेक्षाणां सुखदुःखपुण्यापुण्यविषयाणां
भावनातश्चित्तप्रसादनम् ॥

*maitrī-karunā-muditopekshānām sukha-duhkha-punyāpunya-vishayānām
bhāvanātash citta-prasādanam*

Purity of mind is developed by cultivating
friendship with joyful people, compassion for the sad,
delight towards the pious, and indifference to the sinful.

YS 1.33

According to Patanjali, purity of mind requires the cultivation of specific virtues like friendliness and compassion. But these virtues cannot be cultivated if contrary traits like apathy and hate are present. Therefore, purity of mind requires both the cultivation of desirable virtues and the elimination of undesirable traits and attitudes.

The nature of inner purity, *antahkarana shuddhi*, is best understood by examining the impurities or *ashuddi* that are to be removed. In a Vedantic sense, mental impurity is anything that obstructs your discovery of the true self, *ātmā*. In less technical terms, impurity is anything that disturbs or hinders the normal, healthy functioning of your mind. Such impurities include resentment, anger, hurt, anxiety, and so on. Based on our prior discussion, it is clear that *antahkarana shuddhi* requires emotional growth and maturity.

Shankara states that emotional maturity is an indispensable prerequisite for the study of Vedanta. In a small text named Tattvabodha, he identifies six distinct aspects of emotional maturity:

shama — tranquility, inner harmony
dama — self-control, discipline, restraint
uparati — detachment, freedom from expectations
titikshā — tolerance, patience, acceptance
shraddhā — faith, trust in scriptures and guru
samādhāna — attentiveness, contemplative disposition

Cultivating these six qualities involves a process of emotional growth. This process is not a trivial undertaking. It requires radical transformation of the immature and detrimental ways we think and feel. It seems far easier to change the world around us than to fundamentally change our patterns of thinking and feeling. Developing all six of the above qualities and removing habitual, dysfunctional patterns of thinking is a huge challenge.

To meet this challenge, we need all the help we can get. Fortunately, meditation is tremendously beneficial in this regard. In the Bhagavad Gita, Sri Krishna says:

उपविश्यासने युञ्ज्याद्योगमात्मविशुद्धये ।

upavishyāsane yunjyād yogam ātma-vishuddhaye

Being seated, meditation should be practiced to purify the mind.

BG 6.12

(Note: *ātmā* in this verse refers to the mind, not the true self. Our minds need purification, not *ātmā* which remains untainted by mental activities and is thus eternally pure.)

Meditation can help you cultivate the above-mentioned virtues and gain increased emotional maturity. The teachings and techniques presented in this chapter are meant to support you through that process and help you develop *antahkarana shuddhi.*

Samskāras – Patterns of Thinking

The study of psychology in the West is over one-hundred years old, yet the *rishi*s discovered valuable psychological insights thousands of years ago. One of their insights is about *samskāras*, the mental impressions or conditioning that remain in the wake of experience.

Every experience leaves a *samskāra*, a trace or impression on your mind, like footprints left on a sandy beach. If the same experience occurs several times, the impression will grow deeper, forming what could be called a mental groove or channel. Subsequent thoughts are more likely to fall into this mental groove just like hikers are more likely to tread a well-traveled footpath instead of a rarely used one. By channeling your thoughts, *samskāra*s give rise to habitual patterns of thinking.

A traditional metaphor compares *samskāra*s to the ravines or canyons formed by streams flowing across the land. As water flows down a stream bed over many centuries, it gradually carves a deeper and deeper channel into the ground. And as the channel grows deeper, it can collect additional water, thereby helping it carve even more deeply into the earth. The constant flow of water over thousands and millions of years can cut through solid rock. The magnificent Grand Canyon in Arizona was carved in this way.

The Grand Canyon

Over millions of years, the mighty Colorado River has carved deeply into the earth while geologic forces drove the area upwards. The resulting canyon is nearly 300 miles long and more than one mile deep in places.

If habitual patterns of thinking are as deeply etched into our minds as the Grand Canyon, how can we even hope to change them? The Colorado River could never escape from the towering walls of the canyon. But if it were somehow necessary to change its route, this colossal task could be accomplished by redirecting the river's course *before* it enters the canyon. By redirecting its flow, the river could bypass the canyon entirely. Then over millions of years, it would eventually carve a new canyon for itself.

This metaphor suggests a practical strategy for changing our *samskāras*, our habitual patterns of thinking. Often, the best way to break a bad habit is to replace it with a better one. For example, instead of reaching for a cigarette, a smoker could nibble on a carrot instead. In the same way, we can remove undesirable patterns of thinking by replacing them with desirable new ones.

Scientists have only recently come to understand that habitual patterns of thinking are actually wired into the neurons of our brains. Due to a mechanism called neuroplasticity, repetitive thoughts and behaviors slowly produce physical changes in our brains. Repeated triggering or firing of a particular group of neurons trains them to fire together. This results in the creation of a new mental groove or channel—a new *samskāra*. If a different group of neurons is deliberately triggered again and again, a new *samskāra* can be formed. This attribute of our brains is exploited by certain meditation techniques to create beneficial new patterns of thinking.

Cultivating New Attitudes – *Pratipaksha Bhāvana*

In ancient India, neurons and neuroplasticity were unknown. But the principle of creating beneficial new *samskāra*s by training one's mind was widely employed to facilitate spiritual and emotional growth. Patanjali's use of this principle is seen in the following *sutra*:

वितर्कबाधने प्रतिपक्षभावनम् ॥
vitarka-bādhane pratipaksha-bhāvanam

When undesirable thoughts intrude,
contrary thoughts should be cultivated.

YS 2.33

Here, Patanjali refers to *pratipaksha bhāvana*, a meditation technique used to remove undesirable thoughts and attitudes.

It belongs to the third of the four basic categories of techniques—*contemplation*. As noted earlier, such techniques use specific kinds of thought and reflection to change our patterns of thinking. Instead of focusing on an object of meditation as in *concentration* or passively witnessing the activities of our minds as in *observation*, these techniques invoke particular thoughts and emotions to create desirable new *samskāras*.

Pratipaksha bhāvana is one such technique. It involves cultivating an attitude (*bhāvana*) which is opposed (*pratipaksha*) to an attitude which is to be removed. It is like an antidote for the poisons that can afflict your mind, poisons like anger, hurt, sadness, and self-pity. A specific antidote is needed according to the mental poison to be removed. For example, to remove hate or anger, you should cultivate love and compassion. To eliminate hurt and resentment, you should cultivate forgiveness and understanding. To get rid of sadness or self-pity, you should cultivate happiness and contentment.

A superb application of *pratipaksha bhāvana* is found in an important technique known as *maitrī upāsana*—meditation (*upāsana*) on compassion and friendliness (*maitrī*). This technique helps remove ill-feelings towards anyone by cultivating love and compassion for all. Instructions for the practice of *maitrī upāsana* follows.

157

Exercise 7-1

Maitrī Upāsana – Meditation on Compassion

Preparation:

Following the steps in Exercise 1-1, sit with proper posture, close your eyes, make a *sankalpa* to set aside your concerns, and perform the progressive relaxation exercise.

Practice – Part 1:

Reflect on members of your family. Visualize them, seeing their smiling faces with your mind. Allow yourself to feel tenderness and love towards each of them. Next, reflect on the illness, loss, and other tragedies each of them have suffered in life. Allow yourself to feel sorrow and compassion for them. Take at least five minutes to complete these steps. Finally, recite the following mantra three or more times (see Appendix A for an explanation of this mantra):

लोकाः समस्ताः सुखिनो भवन्तु ॥
lokās samastās sukhino bhavantu
May all people be happy.

Practice – Part 2:

Instead of your family, reflect on close friends and relatives. Perform each of the steps described in Part 1—visualize them, feel tenderness and love towards them, reflect on their suffering, and feel compassion for them. Take at least five minutes for these steps. Finally, recite the above mantra three or more times.

Practice – Part 3:

Next, reflect on people in your neighborhood, city, country, and other countries. Reflect especially on those affected by violence, war, and natural disasters like floods, earthquakes, drought, and famine. Perform each of the steps described in Part 1, taking at least five minutes for these steps. Finally, recite the above mantra.

Practice – Part 4:

Reflect on a particular person that you happen to dislike. Visualize the person, seeing his or her face with your mind. Then reflect on the illness, loss, and other tragedies he or she has suffered in life. Imagine these sufferings as vividly as possible. Allow yourself to feel sorrow and compassion for the person. Take at least five minutes for these steps. Finally, recite the above mantra.

Conclusion:

Hold all the people you just reflected upon in your mind and heart and pray for their happiness and well-being. Then recite the above mantra until you are ready to finish your session.

Half Empty or Half Full

Our attitudes towards life mold all our experiences and shape every event. We commonly say that optimistic people see a glass of water as being half full, while pessimists see it as half empty. Those with cheerful, confident attitudes see each day as a wonderful opportunity to enjoy Ishvara's glorious creation. But those with gloomy, cynical attitudes find each day dreary, difficult, and even threatening. Attitude makes all the difference, and our attitudes are a product of our *samskāras*.

To understand the far-reaching effects of our *samskāras*, the following story will be helpful. Suppose a married couple visits an art museum and stands before an exquisite painting created by a world-renowned artist. The wife marvels at the artwork's great beauty — its rich colors, sensitive subjects, and harmonious sentiments. Her husband, on the other hand, stands with his face inches away from the canvas and remarks that the thick paint has become riddled with tiny black cracks. He then complains that the museum's conservators are doing an awful job of preserving the artworks. From the husband's vantage point, he is unable to appreciate the painting's beauty. He quite literally cannot see the whole picture.

We see what we look for. If we look for beauty in life, we will find it in abundance. But if we look for problems and defects, we will find no shortage of them. Some people are predisposed, either by training or by inclination, to look for problems. For example, engineers are trained to solve technical problems and doctors are trained to diagnose illness, not wellness. Many others are simply critical by nature. Their attention seems drawn to seek out imperfections in anything and anyone.

People with critical, analytical dispositions are said to have proofreader's minds. A proofreader can read a delightful novel from cover to cover, finding many misspellings and punctuation errors, but without enjoying a single word. We all have a little bit of proofreader in us. To the extent this disposition is present, we will focus on what's wrong with the world and our lives instead of appreciating our many blessings.

Fortunately, this is another situation in which *pratipaksha bhāvana*—cultivating opposing attitudes—can be helpful. Proofreader's mind can be overcome by reflecting on the good things in life and appreciating the many wonderful people and events that have blessed us. The antidote for proofreader's mind is the attitude of gratitude. Gratitude helps eliminate the tendency to only look at what is wrong. Cultivating gratitude can create a beneficial new *samskāra* that can lead you to recognize all that is beautiful, meaningful, and sacred in life.

Rather than focusing narrowly on what's wrong—like the man looking at the painting's imperfections—you can metaphorically step back from the details of life to see the whole picture. Instead of concentrating narrowly on today's problems and concerns, you can gain an entirely different perspective by contemplating the entire span of your life. From that perspective, you can appreciate the splendor of life like the woman who admired the painting. The painting was beautiful in spite of its cracks; the defects did not detract from its beauty. Likewise, in spite of your many problems and difficulties, there is a great deal to appreciate in your life. You can find so much to be grateful for if you look for it.

The following meditation exercise is intended to cultivate gratitude as an antidote for the tendency of always looking for what is wrong in life.

Exercise 7-2

Meditation on Gratitude

Preparation:

Following the steps in Exercise 1-1, sit with proper posture, close your eyes, make a *sankalpa* to set aside your concerns, and perform the progressive relaxation exercise.

Practice – Part 1:

Reflect on your childhood. Mentally picture your childhood home and your parents, siblings, friends, and relatives, noticing how young they looked then. Next, recall the happiest events of your childhood—family holidays, birthdays, festivals, etc. Allow yourself to feel some of the joy and excitement you felt then. Finally, reflect on how fortunate you were to have been born in such a wonderful, loving family.

Take at least five minutes to complete these steps, then recite the following mantra three or more times (see Appendix A for an explanation of this mantra):

धन्योऽहं धन्योऽहं धन्योऽहं अहं धन्यः ॥

dhanyo'ham dhanyo'ham dhanyo'ham aham dhanyah

Blessed am I, blessed am I, blessed am I, I am blessed!

Practice – Part 2:

Reflect on the education you received in school, high school, college, etc. and any favorite teachers you might still remember. Consider how those years of learning molded your mind and opened many doors for you, contributing to future happiness and prosperity for you and your family. Bear in mind that many people are denied such opportunities for learning. Finally, reflect with gratitude on the many blessings in life you received as a result of your education.

Take at least five minutes to complete these steps, then recite the above mantra three or more times.

Practice – Part 3:

Reflect on your family, relatives, and friends as they are today, picturing them in your mind. Reflect on the love, friendship, care, and support you have received from them. Consider how empty your life would be without them. Finally, reflect with gratitude on how blessed you are to have each of them in your life today.

Take at least five minutes to complete these steps, then recite the above mantra three or more times.

Practice – Part 4:

Reflect on the most wonderful events in your life—births, graduations, promotions, marriages, etc. Reflect on how much joy and contentment you have received as a result of these events, bearing in mind that many people are denied such opportunities. Finally, allow yourself to feel profoundly grateful for each of these many blessings.

Take at least five minutes to complete these steps, then recite the above mantra until you are ready to conclude this meditation.

Widening Your Perspective on Life

Each day, you are assaulted by a multitude of problems that can drain your energy and consume your attention. Because of this, you can become so engrossed in the pesky details of life that you lose sight of the big picture, like the man in the art museum. Managers sometimes complain that their staff is so busy attending to urgent problems that no one is available to perform the everyday work. If every worker is busy putting out fires, as they say, who will pay the bills or answer the phone?

You can become so preoccupied with life's problems that you lose sight of what is truly important. Your treasured goals, your hopes and dreams, and your core values can all be temporarily forgotten when urgent situations demand your full attention. Your priorities can be particularly disturbed at times of great emotional pain. Intense sorrow or grief can throw your life off-balance, leaving you disoriented and confused about life's meaning and purpose.

What is the meaning and purpose of life? The ancient *rishi*s answered this weighty question with amazing clarity and brevity. They enumerated four primary goals of life, the four *purushārtha*s:

dharma – righteousness
artha – wealth and security
kāma – pleasure
moksha – liberation, enlightenment

The *rishis* understood that life is a gift from Ishvara, a gift of God to be treasured and enjoyed. Therefore *kāma* and *artha*, pleasure and wealth, are considered essential and legitimate goals of life. They are legitimate so long as they are pursued in conformance with the principles of dharma, which is the first of the four goals. The *rishis* also recognized that the pursuit of dharma, *artha*, and *kāma* cannot produce perfect peace or uninterrupted contentment. For this reason, they declared *moksha*, liberation or enlightenment, to be the highest of the four goals.

All four of these goals are to be pursued throughout life, but their relative importance can shift from time to time as your priorities change. For example, *artha* and *kāma* might assume greater importance early in life. Later on, the pursuit of *moksha* may gain precedence. Life is fluid, ever-changing, so it is inevitable that your priorities will also change. Your goals are like moving targets, so it is necessary to re-examine your priorities continually.

However, when you are thrown off-balance by a crisis or tragedy, you can easily lose sight of your goals and get confused about priorities. Some people's lives are thrown into complete disarray after suffering a great loss like the death of a loved one or losing a job. In the chaos and confusion of such crises, some people react rashly. Some leave their families. Some turn to alcohol or drugs. Some even consider taking their lives. If major catastrophes can lead to such recklessness, then lesser misfortunes can certainly distort your judgment and lead you to make inappropriate decisions.

What can be done to maintain objectivity and keep priorities straight, even in times of crisis? As previously discussed, you can learn to step back and see the big picture. You can do so by reflecting on the entire span of your life, from beginning to end, from birth to death. With this wide perspective, goals and priorities can come into focus with surprising clarity.

For example, imagine yourself at the age of ninety, looking back on your life. From that perspective, would you wish you had worked harder at your profession or waited longer before retirement? Probably not. Would you wish you had spent more time watching television and surfing the internet? Certainly not.

On the other hand, you might indeed wish you had spent more time with your loved ones. You might wish you had been more adventurous and traveled more. You might wish you had been more kind, loving, and generous. From this discussion, you can sense the tremendous value of reflecting on your entire life as a way to broaden your perspective and clarify your priorities.

When you see an exquisite old painting in a museum, the painting's chips, cracks, and other defects do not detract even a bit from its marvelous beauty. Why? Because the defects are tiny relative to the size of the entire painting. Similarly, your struggles, failures, and losses do not detract from the beauty and profundity of your life. Those defects are equally tiny when viewed with respect to your entire lifespan, from birth to death.

The following meditation exercise will help you gain a wide perspective on your life to appreciate it fully and to clarify your goals and priorities. You will be guided to reflect on your life from a point near the time of your death. If thinking about your own death makes you uncomfortable, you may skip this exercise.

Exercise 7-3

End of Life Meditation

Preparation:

Following the steps in Exercise 1-1, sit with proper posture, close your eyes, make a *sankalpa* to set aside your concerns, and perform the progressive relaxation exercise.

Practice – Part 1:

Imagine yourself at the age of ninety, preparing to depart this life. Picture yourself laying in bed, comfortable, pain-free, clear-minded, and surrounded by loved ones. Imagine yourself feeling utterly content, satisfied that you have lived a long, wonderful life, and eager to reflect on your entire lifespan before you leave this world.

Begin by reflecting on the first two decades of your life. Recall your childhood home, your parents, siblings, and friends. Recall significant events and milestones in your life during those years. After several minutes of reflection, recite the following mantra three or more times. If you have a mantra you use regularly, you may recite it instead.

ॐ नमो नारायणाय ॥

om namo nārāyanāya

Om! Salutations to Narayana, the Lord who preserves all.

Practice – Parts 2 to 8:

Reflect on each succeeding decade of your adult life—your twenties, thirties, forties, fifties, sixties, seventies, and eighties—one decade at a time. When you reach your current age, simply imagine the events that might occur in the coming decades.

For each decade, recall where you lived and picture your loved ones and others in your life. Recall significant events like graduations, marriages, births, deaths, moving, etc. Recall the challenges you faced and the accomplishments you achieved. Recall important decisions you made and reflect on how they shaped your life. After several minutes of reflection, recite the above mantra three or more times, then proceed to the next decade.

Conclusion:

After reflecting on your final decade and reciting the mantra, offer a prayer of gratitude for all the wonderful people and experiences in your life. Then, resolve to live the remaining years of your life as fully and wisely as possible. Finally, recite the mantra until you are ready to finish this meditation.

CHAPTER EIGHT

DEVOTIONAL MEDITATION: *UPĀSANA*

In this chapter we come to the last of the four basic categories of meditation. Having already discussed techniques based on concentration, observation, and contemplation, we will now explore techniques based on devotion, *bhakti*. These prayerful meditation practices are generally known as *upāsana*.

The *rishis* considered *bhakti* or devotion to be just as important as meditation. The Kaivalya Upanishad puts faith and devotion side by side with meditation as the principal means for gaining spiritual truth:

श्रद्धाभक्तिध्यानयोगादवैहि ।

shraddhā-bhakti-dhyāna-yogād avaihi

Know it (*brahman*, ultimate reality) through
the practice of faith, devotion, and meditation.

KaiU 2

In the Hindu tradition, prayer and worship have always been considered essential in spiritual life. Such practices are part of a vast devotional realm that remains mostly unexplored by the central teachings of Vedanta. Vedanta primarily engages our intellects, not our emotions. Yet emotion is an important and powerful aspect of our nature. To reach the lofty goal of enlightenment requires extraordinary effort, so we must employ every resource at our disposal, including our emotions. The devotional practices of *bhakti* actively engage our emotions for the sake of spiritual growth.

Devotional meditation or *upāsana* is a unique practice because it brings prayer and meditation together. Its prayerful aspect introduces an entirely new dimension to meditation — a personal relationship and emotional connection with Ishvara, the God of all. As a form of prayer, *upāsana* invokes Ishvara's grace. Considering how difficult it is to discipline our minds and focus our attention, we can certainly benefit from God's grace at the time of meditation.

In Chapter Three, we noted that a suitable object of meditation must be selected for *dhāranā* and *dhyāna*, concentration and meditation. Suitable objects include sounds, breath, mantras, and so on. In *upāsana*, Ishvara becomes the object of meditation on which our attention is focused. Patanjali declares the importance of meditating on Ishvara in the following *sutra*:

समाधिसिद्धिरीश्वरप्रणिधानात् ॥

samādhi-siddhir īshvara-pranidhānāt

Samādhi can be gained by concentration on Ishvara.

YS 2.45

Samādhi is the eighth and final limb of yoga. In Patanjali's system of meditation, it is the ultimate goal. Even though *samādhi* can be reached by meditating on other suitable objects, Patanjali emphasizes meditation on Ishvara in this *sutra*. He

170

thus acknowledges the importance of incorporating devotion into the practice of meditation.

In the sixth chapter of the Bhagavad Gita where Sri Krishna teaches Arjuna how to meditate, detailed instructions on posture, concentration, and mental discipline are given. Sri Krishna also prescribes a particular object of meditation for Arjuna to concentrate upon. That object is clearly identified when Sri Krishna says:

मनः संयम्य मच्चित्तो युक्त आसीत मत्परः ।

manah samyamya maccitto yukta āsīta matparah

Having restrained your mind, fix your attention on Me.
Remain focused on Me.

BG 6.14

In this verse, Arjuna is directed to meditate on Sri Krishna himself. Of course, Sri Krishna is an incarnation of Vishnu, an aspect of Ishvara. So, to meditate on Sri Krishna is to meditate on Ishvara.

This verse should not be construed to suggest that we should meditate only on Sri Krishna. Hinduism recognizes many forms in which we can worship Ishvara, such as Shiva, Lakshmi, Ganesha, and so on. Some people develop a deep connection to one of these forms which becomes the focal point of their devotion. That special form is called *ishta devatā*, one's chosen (*ishta*) form of God (*devatā*).

In this verse, Arjuna is actually instructed to meditate on his own *ishta devatā* which happens to be Sri Krishna. In the practice of *upāsana*, you should similarly meditate on your own *ishta devatā*. If there is no particular form of Ishvara to which you feel especially drawn, you may choose any deity for your practice.

Relationship with Ishvara

The foundation for both prayer and *upāsana* is establishing a personal relationship with Ishvara. Without such a relationship, the deep emotional connection that lies at the heart of all devotional practices cannot develop. One who develops this connection to Ishvara is called a *bhakta,* a devotee.

Every *bhakta* develops his or her own unique relationship with Ishvara. Relationships are based on feelings, not on philosophical truths or religious doctrines. Therefore, there are no correct or incorrect relationships; emotional bonding depends on each individual. In fact, scriptural stories about celebrated *bhakta*s demonstrate a wide range of moods, attitudes, and symbolic associations with regards to Ishvara.

In general, these relationships fall into two broad categories: *aishvarya* and *mādhurya*. *Aishvarya* means majesty. It describes relationships in which we appreciate the magnificence of the all-pervasive, all-powerful, all-knowing God of the universe. *Mādhurya*, on the other hand, means sweetness. It describes a tender, loving, intimate relationship with Ishvara who loves and accepts us unconditionally. The practice of *upāsana* can be based on either or both of these relationships.

Upāsana provides an opportunity to spend some time with Ishvara, so to speak. Even if you believe that Ishvara is ever-present, you probably do not feel that presence constant-ly. The practice of *upāsana* can help you sense Ishvara's divine presence at any time. It can also help you develop a deeper emotional connection or closeness with Ishvara.

Emotional closeness can be a source of great comfort and support. You find this whenever you share your joys and troubles with loved ones who understand and accept you unconditionally. Even if they cannot solve your problems, they are ready to share your emotional burdens. When burdens are shared, they feel much lighter. You gain strength and courage to cope with difficulties by sharing your troubles, and by sharing your joys, your happiness seems magnified.

Just as you share your joys and troubles with loved ones, you can share them with Ishvara. You are completely understood and unconditionally accepted by Ishvara, infinitely more so than by your dearest friend. You can find immense support when you open your heart to Ishvara and share your experiences, happy or sad. *Upāsana* can be an opportunity for such sharing.

In another way, *upāsana* can be likened to visiting your dear parents. As a child, you wanted your parents to give you many things. Now as an adult, you just want to be in their loving presence. This metaphor nicely describes the practice of *upāsana*. Instead of praying to Ishvara for specific intentions, you can simply sit quietly in meditation, feeling Ishvara's sacred, loving presence.

When you are with loved ones, you feel loved even if they do not say anything. Even without seeing them, you feel loved. When you were a child lying in bed at night, just knowing your parents were in a nearby room made you feel safe and loved. Similarly, with your eyes closed and without even uttering a prayer, you can feel Ishvara's loving presence in *upāsana*.

As a child, you felt loved even when you did not see or hear your parents because you *knew* they loved you. Even when they punished you for misbehaving, you never doubted their unceasing love. Your parents' love for you is a fitting metaphor for Ishvara's unconditional love and acceptance. The celebrated Bengali poet, Rabindranath Tagore, composed the following verse which sensitively conveys the feeling of Ishvara's unconditional love and acceptance:

Accept me, my Lord, accept me for this while.

Let those orphaned days that passed without Thee be forgotten. Only spread this little moment wide across Thy lap, holding it under Thy light.

I have wandered in pursuit of voices that drew me yet led me nowhere. Now let me sit in peace and listen to Thy words in the soul of my silence.

Do not turn away Thy face from my heart's dark secrets, but burn them till they are alight with Thy fire.

Rabindranath Tagore: Crossings

Tagore describes *upāsana* perfectly where he says, "Now let me sit in peace and listen to Thy words in the soul of my silence."

If you planned a special visit with your parents, you would never think of bringing a casual acquaintance with you. That person's presence would be distracting and inappropriate. In a similar way, when you plan to spend time with Ishvara in meditation, you want to be free from distractions, especially distractions created by your own mind. For this reason, it is helpful to use a technique that can quiet your mind during the practice of *upāsana*.

Of all the techniques described thus far, mantra *japa* is perhaps best-suited for this purpose. Since mantras are prayers as well as objects of meditation, they are ideal for the practice of *upāsana*. For the meditation exercise below, choose a mantra addressed to your *ishta devatā*. If there is no special form of Ishvara to which you are particularly drawn, you may choose any mantra from Appendix A.

Exercise 8-1

Being in the Presence of Ishvara

Preparation:

Following the steps in Exercise 1-1, sit with proper posture, close your eyes, make a sankalpa to set aside your concerns, and perform the progressive relaxation exercise.

Practice:

Remind yourself that you have set this time aside specifically to be in Ishvara's sacred presence. Begin reciting your mantra as in Exercise 4-2, Silent Mantra *Japa*. As you recite the mantra, allow yourself to be emotionally open and receptive as you would with a close family member or dear friend. Recognize that your sorrows, failures, mistakes, and shortcomings are fully understood by Ishvara who loves and accepts you unconditionally. Continue for ten minutes or more.

From time to time, stop reciting the mantra and allow yourself to silently appreciate Ishvara's sacred presence. When your mind starts to wander, resume recitation of the mantra.

Options:

Before beginning this meditation exercise, slowly read the above-quoted poem of Rabindranath Tagore one or more times.

Imagery and Symbolism

Looking at certain images can affect us profoundly, like looking at photos of family members when traveling far from home. Our feelings can also be stirred when we stand before a temple's altar and gaze at beautiful, consecrated deities lovingly adorned with fine dress and garlands of fresh flowers. Sights like these can touch our hearts and draw out our emotions.

We can also see images in our minds. We all have the ability to visualize, to imagine forms and images. This visual ability can be of great benefit in the practice of *upāsana*. Your experience of emotional closeness with Ishvara can be enhanced by envisioning the particular form of Ishvara you are meditating upon.

Holding a sacred image in your mind not only engages your emotions, it also provides a superb object of meditation on which you can concentrate your attention. The image becomes the focal point of yogic *dhāranā* and *dhyāna*. Some meditators find it easier to restrain their minds from wandering when they envision the deity to which their mantra is addressed. This practice can be made even more effective by picturing the deity as vividly as possible and by reflecting on the deity's symbolism.

Traditional images of Hindu deities are rich with symbolism. The details of posture, dress, arms, hands, etc. are based on scriptural descriptions found in Puranic texts and elsewhere. However, some contemporary artists have departed from these traditional depictions. They take considerable liberty in how they portray deities, such as depicting Ganesha playing tabla drums. When you choose an image for meditation, it may be helpful to look at the exquisitely sculpted deities found in temples. The artisans who carve those forms are highly skilled and their work is based on traditional scriptural descriptions.

Another good source of imagery is the scriptural descriptions themselves. They are mostly found in *dhyāna shloka*s, verses (*shloka*s) that describe a particular deity for the sake of meditation (*dhyāna*). For each deity, many *dhyāna shloka*s have been composed. Their depictions range from simple to elaborate and can differ somewhat from one to another. These *dhyāna shloka*s are meant to be recited before worship or meditation to establish the deity's image in your mind. *Dhyāna shloka*s for various deities can be found in Appendix A.

Every depiction of a deity—whether in a *dhyāna shloka*, sculpted form, or colorful picture—makes extensive use of symbolism. Unfortunately, much of that symbolism can remain unrecognized or be misunderstood due to its subtlety and complexity. This is a great loss because each detail of a deity abounds with aesthetic beauty, symbolic meaning, and importance for prayer and meditation.

Symbolism can have tremendous power. Due to symbolism, a piece of cloth can invoke strong patriotic feelings when it happens to be your country's national flag. A piece of paper acquires great monetary value if it happens to be a one-hundred dollar bill. If you could not recognize the flag or banknote, they would have no value to you. Symbols acquire power only when their symbolism is understood. For this reason, it is important to understand the symbolism of the particular deity you meditate upon.

From a Vedantic standpoint, symbolism can be described as intentional superimposition. A nation's greatness is deliberately superimposed on its flag, just as monetary value is superimposed on a banknote. In the Hindu tradition, various aspects of Ishvara's power and glory are deliberately superimposed on each deity. For example, Ishvara's power to remove obstacles is superimposed on Ganesha, and the power to sustain the universe is superimposed on Vishnu. Due to symbolism, a sacred form on an altar becomes suitable for worship and a sacred image held in your mind becomes suitable for meditation.

The following meditation exercise makes use of symbolism. Before practice, some preparation is necessary. First, select a mantra addressed to your *ishta devatā* or a deity of your choice. Then, study a picture or sculpted form of that deity so you can envision it clearly in your mind. Find a *dhyāna shloka* for the deity and learn its meaning. Become familiar with the symbolism of the deity and learn the significance of each symbol. *Dhyāna shloka*s and brief explanations of symbolism for various deities are included in Appendix A.

Exercise 8-2

Japa with Visualization

Preparation:

Following the steps in Exercise 1-1, sit with proper posture, close your eyes, make a *sankalpa* to set aside your concerns, and perform the progressive relaxation exercise.

Practice – Part 1:

Begin by reciting the *dhyāna shloka* for the deity you selected and reflect on its meaning. Envision the deity depicted by the verse as vividly as possible. Reflect on each of its details along with the related symbolism.

Practice – Part 2:

Begin silent recitation of the deity's mantra, following the directions in Exercise 4-2, Silent Mantra *Japa*. Maintain the deity's image clearly in your mind throughout this practice. Continue for ten minutes or more.

Options:

Before reciting the mantra, imagine yourself entering a magnificent temple and standing before a beautiful altar on which your chosen deity resides. Visualize the deity on that altar, splendidly dressed, adorned with jewels, and garlanded with fresh flowers.

Temple of the Heart

Sacred forms of Ishvara can be found on altars in homes and temples around the world. Yet Hindu scriptures teach that Ishvara actually pervades the universe, residing in all things and every being, thereby rendering them divine. That very

Ishvara resides in you as well. For this reason, just as you can meditate on Ishvara's form on an altar, you can also meditate on Ishvara's presence in yourself, on the altar of your heart.

Vedanta teaches that Ishvara is present in everything as the source of existence and consciousness. Our physical bodies pulsing with life exist due to Ishvara's presence. Our powerful minds and the consciousness shining within them owe their very existence to Ishvara's sacred presence. Here again, to thoroughly explore profound Vedantic teachings such as these is beyond the scope of this book. In this section, we will focus on Ishvara's presence in a manner helpful for the practice of *upāsana*.

Many scriptures declare that Ishvara dwells in our hearts. In the Bhagavad Gita, Sri Krishna says:

ईश्वरः सर्वभूतानां हृद्देशेऽर्जुन तिष्ठति ।

īshvarah sarva-bhūtānām hrid-deshe 'rjuna tishthati

O Arjuna, Ishvara dwells in the hearts of all creatures.

BG 18.61

In this verse, "heart" refers not to a physical organ but to the center of your existence, the innermost core of your being. Ishvara abides within, blessing you with existence and consciousness.

A traditional metaphor depicts your body as a temple and your heart as an altar at the center of the temple. Upon the altar of your heart, Ishvara resides as the temple's consecrated deity. The aptness of this lovely image is no accident—the architecture of most temples is based on this very idea. Temples are actually designed to represent Ishvara's presence in our hearts. In ancient times, the most common word for temple was *devālaya*, Ishvara's abode. Such an abode could be in a person's body as well as in a building.

Temple architecture is based on symbolism that will become apparent if we examine the layout of a typical temple as shown in the following diagram.

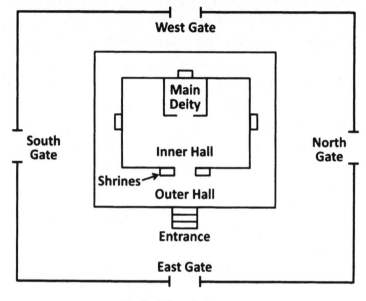

Typical Temple Layout

The layout above is representative of many large South Indian temples. Such temples are usually enclosed by one or more outer walls containing huge, elaborately sculpted gateways called *gopurams*. Worshipers enter the temple compound through one of the gateways and proceed to the temple's outer hall. There, they offer prayers at shrines before proceeding to the smaller inner hall. Finally, they come to the innermost part of the temple, the sacred chamber or *garbhagriha* where the main deity resides.

To enter a temple for worship symbolically represents a form of *upāsana* in which you meditate on Ishvara's presence within yourself. The temple's outer wall represents your body's periphery; its four gateways represent your eyes, ears, nose, and mouth. Entering the temple's outer and inner halls represents turning your attention away from the world and directing it within yourself. Praying to the deity in the *garbhagriha* represents meditating on Ishvara's presence in your heart. Just as the *garbhagriha* is the innermost part of a temple, your heart is the innermost part of your being.

The particular deity installed in a *garbhagriha* is specially chosen for each temple. In a similar way, you are free to choose the form and manner in which you envision Ishvara's presence in yourself. If it is helpful, you can imagine your *ishta devatā* or any deity as being physically present in your heart. This form of visualization is widely used and is prescribed in several scriptures, including the Katha Upanishad:

अङ्गुष्ठमात्रः पुरुषोऽन्तरात्मा सदा जनानां हृदये संनिविष्टः ।

angushtha-mātrah purusho 'ntarātmā sadā janānām hridaye sannivishtah

The Supreme Being, having the size of a thumb,
is forever present in people's hearts as their inner self.

KaU 6.17

"Having the size of a thumb" is a poetic way of describing a deity's physical form as being small enough to reside in your heart.

Many other kinds of visualization have been prescribed in the scriptures, such as imagining Ishvara's presence as a small flame shining in your heart. This imagery is expressed in the soaring verses of the Narayana Suktam, an extraordinary hymn to Vishnu from the Yajur Veda. The following passage is adapted from the hymn:

> *Meditate on the limitless, unchanging, omniscient Lord dwelling in your heart like a lotus bud hanging down between your throat and navel, surrounded by nerves, and shining brightly. In the tiny space within the bud, a fire blazes. Flames spread every-*

where, radiating sideways and above, warming your body from head to feet.

Ishvara is like a tiny tongue of fire among the flames, slender as a grain and bright as the lightning from dark clouds. In the midst of those flames, He abides as the supreme Self. He is Brahma. He is Shiva. He is Vishnu and Indra. He is eternal, supreme, and self-luminous.

Narayana Sukta 6-12

You can meditate on Ishvara's presence in your heart using the imagery above or in any manner that enhances your experience.

Any place of prayer, worship, or meditation should be kept clean and quiet. If you meditate at the altar of your heart, it is your mind that must be clean and quiet. It should not be sullied by hurt, anger, frustration, and the like. The first two limbs of yoga, *yama* and *niyama*, are prescribed by Patanjali specifically to maintain inner purity. These *angas* should be practiced at all times to keep your heart pure and preserve the sanctity of your inner altar.

If children are allowed to run around in a temple and create a ruckus, worshipers will be distracted. Similarly, when noisy thoughts swirl around in your mind during *upāsana*, you will be distracted. The techniques already explained in this book can be used to quiet your mind when you meditate on Ishvara's presence in your heart. The following meditation exercise provides further guidance for this practice.

Exercise 8-3

Ishvara's Presence in Your Heart

Preparation:

Following the steps in Exercise 1-1, sit with proper posture, close your eyes, make a *sankalpa* to set aside your concerns, and perform the progressive relaxation exercise.

Practice – Part 1:

Turn your attention towards your heart. Visualize the presence of Ishvara there as vividly as possible, in any form and manner you choose. Allow yourself to feel a sense of warmth radiating from your heart.

Practice – Part 2:

Begin silently reciting a mantra of your choice following the directions in Exercise 4-2, Silent Mantra *Japa*. Continue to visualize and feel Ishvara's sacred presence in your heart as clearly as possible. Continue for ten minutes or more.

From time to time, stop reciting the mantra and allow yourself to silently appreciate Ishvara's sacred presence in your heart. When your mind starts to wander, resume recitation of the mantra.

Options:

Instead of reciting a mantra, you may practice any meditation technique from the prior chapters that you have found particularly effective in quieting your mind. Recommended practices include *Prāna Vīkshana* (Exercise 1-2), Slow Deep Breathing (Exercise 2-3), and *Ujjayī Prānāyāma* (Exercise 2-4). While performing this technique, continue to visualize and feel Ishvara's sacred presence in your heart as vividly as possible.

A Sacred Place, Within and Without

The first three exercises in this chapter are all intended to help you find or create a meditative place in which you can sense Ishvara's divine presence. That place could be at a beautiful altar or temple, real or imagined. That place could be envisioning yourself at the feet of your *ishta devatā*. Or that place could be within your own heart. Wherever it is, such a place can become an exceedingly sacred and cherished spot for you, perhaps more sacred than any other.

You have probably noticed that various places evoke different feelings. You feel different at your work place than in your living room. You feel different at a supermarket than in a temple. Some places can make you feel uncomfortable or anxious, like a dark alley, while others make you feel relaxed, peaceful, and content.

What is it about a particular place that makes you feel peaceful and content? Would you feel content in your own home or your parents' home if it was unoccupied, entirely vacant? Would you feel peaceful in a temple if its *garbhagriha* was empty? Obviously, what makes these places special is not the building or location, but rather the presence of someone dear to you. In the meditative space of *upāsana*, it is Ishvara's presence that blesses you with peace and contentment.

You may also have noticed that it takes time for a particular place to feel special. When you first move into a new house, it takes a while before it feels like a cozy home. If you set up a new altar, it takes a while before it feels like a sacred place of worship. The special character of such places develops gradually when you return to them again and again. For this reason, each time you return to the meditative space of *upāsana*, your sense of Ishvara's divine presence will grow stronger.

Although you might feel Ishvara's presence more strongly in some places than others, the all-pervasive God of the cosmos abides in all things, everywhere. Yet this sacred presence is somehow hidden. It cannot be perceived with your eyes and ears, nor can it be touched or grasped. Yet Ishvara's presence can indeed be discovered; it can be known. Ishvara's presence is discerned with your mind, not with your senses.

In the Bhagavad Gita, Sri Krishna, speaking as Ishvara, explains how Ishvara pervades all:

मत्तः परतरं नान्यत्किञ्चिदस्ति धनञ्जय ।
मयि सर्वमिदं प्रोतं सूत्रे मणिगणा इव ॥

mattah parataram nānyat kincid asti dhananjaya
mayi sarvam idam protam sūtre manigaṇā iva

O Arjuna, there is nothing here separate from me.
Everything is strung on me like gemstones on a thread.

BG 7.7

According to Sri Krishna, Ishvara is present in everything like the string on which beads of a necklace are strung. The string is hidden within each bead. Likewise, Ishvara is hidden in each thing. Though you cannot see the string, you know it is present. In the same way, you can know that Ishvara is present in every rock, plant, animal, and person.

Ishvara's presence can be recognized anywhere, yet it can be appreciated with special delight in natural settings, amongst the trees, clouds, and chirping birds. Sri Krishna, still speaking as Ishvara in the following passage, describes His presence in nature in this way:

रसोऽहमप्सु कौन्तेय प्रभासि शशिसूर्ययोः ।
पुण्यो गन्धः पृथिव्यां च तेजश्चास्मि विभावसौ ।

raso 'ham apsu kaunteya prabhāsi shashi-sūryayoh
punyo gandhah prithivyām ca tejash cāsmi vibhāvasau

Arjuna, I am the wetness of water and the light of sun and moon. I am the sweet smell of earth and the brilliance of fire.

BG 7.8, 7.9

As discussed in the prior chapter, you see what you look for. When you go outside, you can see soil, stones, and grass. But if you look for Ishvara's presence, you can see it everywhere. That is, you can know or appreciate Ishvara's presence far and wide — as the wetness of water, as the light of the sun, and so on.

The following exercise describes how to take a meditative walk to appreciate Ishvara's presence in nature. When you are surrounded by the glories of nature, you might get the sense that you are walking through Ishvara, so to speak.

Exercise 8-4

Walking through Ishvara

Preparation:

Go to a beautiful place suitable for walking. Make a *sankalpa* to set aside your problems and concerns as in Exercise 1-1. If you are accompanied by someone, agree to remain silent for the duration of the walk.

Practice:

Walk at a comfortable pace, silently reciting a mantra of your choice to keep your mind from wandering. If you like, you can recite it in sync with your footsteps as in Exercise 4-4, Walking *Japa*, beginning each mantra with your right footstep. When your mind wanders, gently bring it back to the mantra.

As you walk, gaze at the sky, trees, flowers, and everything around you, appreciating Ishvara's presence everywhere. Notice the sound of chirping birds and the touch of the sun and wind on your skin, recognizing Ishvara's presence in each of these. Surrounded by nature, allow yourself to feel Ishvara's sacred presence all around you, as though you are walking through Ishvara.

Options:

Stop reciting the mantra and simply appreciate Ishvara's divine presence with your full attention. When your mind starts to wander, resume silent recitation of your mantra.

CHAPTER NINE

GOING DEEPER:
ADVANCED TECHNIQUES

This chapter explores advanced techniques drawn from each of the four basic categories of meditation — *concentration, observation, contemplation,* and *devotion.* The topics covered here touch upon some of the most profound teachings of Vedanta, so extra effort might be required for full comprehension. The techniques described in this chapter are more demanding than those in prior chapters. It is essential to practice the earlier exercises thoroughly before proceeding to those in this chapter. If the material below seems too confusing, or if the exercises seem too difficult, you may skip ahead to the next chapter and return to this chapter at a later date.

We turn first to the concentration-based techniques which were introduced in Chapter Three. This topic brings us to the last of Patanjali's eight limbs of yoga, *samādhi.* Patanjali describes *samādhi* in the following *sutra:*

सर्वार्थतैकाग्रतयोः क्षयोदयौ चित्तस्य समाधिपरिणामः ॥

sarvārthataikāgratayoh kshayodayau cittasya samādhi-parināmah

Withdrawal of attention from everything
and development of one-pointed attention
is the state of mind called *samādhi*.

YS 3.11

To better understand this *sutra* and the concept of one-pointed attention, let us return to the metaphor from Chapter Three that compares your power of attention to a flashlight beam. When a flashlight casts a wide beam, everything in front of it is illumined. Your untrained and unfocused attention is like that wide beam—open to everything. But when a flashlight throws a very narrow beam, one object is illumined while others are cast into darkness. Similarly, when your attention is narrowly concentrated on one thing, everything else gets ignored. All this was seen before when discussing *pratyāhāra* and *dhāranā*, sense withdrawal and concentration.

An additional factor of great importance is introduced by this *sutra*—the development of a one-pointed mind. *Citta ekāgratā*, one-pointedness (*ekāgratā*) of mind (*citta*), is a defining feature of *samādhi*. It is the highest possible degree of concentration. It results from narrowing the focus of attention down to a single point, like a flashlight beam focused to the size of a pinpoint. *Citta ekāgratā* is achieved through copious practice of yoga's first seven limbs. When that practice is sufficient, the eighth limb, *samādhi*, can be reached.

The Bhagavad Gita describes *samādhi* with a wonderful metaphor:

यथा दीपो निवातस्थो नेङ्गते सोपमा स्मृता ।

yathā dīpo nivātastho nengate sopamā smritā

(*Samādhi*) is like a lamp
shielded from the wind that never flickers.

BG 6.19

You have probably seen a flame of a candle or oil lamp appear absolutely motionless, as though painted on space, when there is not the slightest movement of air to disturb it. The shining, unwavering flame represents a mind absorbed in *samādhi,* a brilliant, completely concentrated mind whose attention is unshakably fixed on its object of meditation.

A perfectly steady flame is even more remarkable because it is actually in constant motion, just like the steady stream of oil mentioned in Chapter Four. Within such a flame is a continuous flow of glowing, superheated gas, rising with perfect uniformity. That flow represents the unchanging, seamless flow of *vritti*s during *samādhi.* In this state, each *vritti* is identical and perfectly molded into the form of the object of meditation.

To fully understand *samādhi,* we must abandon the flashlight analogy. *Samādhi* is like replacing a flashlight with a laser. Ordinary light is a random flow of assorted light waves. In a laser beam, however, every wave is identical and precisely aligned. This results in a beam of tremendous power. While a one-hundred watt light bulb can illumine a room, a one-hundred watt laser can burn through solid steel. Such is the mind's power of concentration during *samādhi.*

State of Absorption

Thus far, we have discussed the extraordinary degree of concentration present in *samādhi.* But this state has another, equally important quality – absorption. The meditator becomes absorbed in the object of meditation during *samādhi*. Between the meditator and object of meditation, there ordinarily exists a clear distinction, a separation, a kind of mental distance. But that distance decreases as *samādhi* is approached and finally reaches zero when the meditator becomes absorbed in the object of meditation. Then, the object of meditation alone remains.

Patanjali describes this remarkable condition in the following *sutra*:

तदेवार्थमात्रनिर्भासं स्वरूपशून्यमिव समाधिः ॥

tad evārtha-mātra-nirbhāsam svarūpa-shūnyam iva samādhih

When the object of meditation alone appears
and the meditator seems to be absent, that is *samādhi*.

YS 3.3

In *samādhi*, only the object of meditation remains; the meditator seems to disappear. How can that happen? Such an experience is not so strange as you might imagine. Have you ever gazed into a pitch-black sky filled with thousands of shining stars and felt yourself somehow slipping away? Or have you ever listened to music so breathtaking that you found yourself getting lost in it? In experiences like these, a kind of absorption occurs.

When you get lost while listening to your favorite music, you can still hear and enjoy it. So who gets lost? In Vedantic terms, the one who disappears during such experiences is the ego or *ahankāra*. The word *ego* is Latin for the pronoun "I" and *ahankāra* literally means the maker (*kāra*) of I (*aham*). These terms refer to the sense of individuality you feel most of the time—your sense of I-ness.

When you get lost in music, your *ahankāra* or feeling of I-ness disappears temporarily. Your *ahankāra* also disappears in *samādhi* when your sense of being a meditator fades away. In that state, the object of meditation continues to be experienced in the absence of your usual feeling of I-ness.

This extraordinary state seems to involve a strange paradox. Meditation requires considerable effort, and such effort requires lots of willpower. Without willful effort, meditation cannot take place. But your willpower itself fades along with your *ahankāra* in a state of absorption. For instance, when you are absorbed in music, you can't do anything. You cannot walk or talk; you can't even think. You can only enjoy the experience. In the same way, while you are absorbed in *samādhi*, you cannot willfully do anything. You cannot focus your attention, watch your breath, or recite a mantra. Then how can you continue to meditate?

As previously noted, your mind can perform many tasks automatically, without willpower. When driving a car, for example, you do not require willful effort to press the brake pedal as you approach a stop sign. You do it automatically. Willpower is not required because your mind is well-trained to drive a car safely. In the same way, when your mind is well-trained to perform a particular meditation technique, it can automatically maintain the technique during *samādhi*, even without your willful effort.

Your willpower is needed to practice any technique. But since your will is absent while you are absorbed in *samādhi*, you cannot actually practice *samādhi*. It cannot be practiced because it is not a technique. *Samādhi* is the goal of yoga, not something to be practiced. *Samādhi* is a state you can reach with proper effort. Through your willful practice of the first seven *angas* of yoga, you can reach the eighth, *samādhi*.

The following meditation exercise describes how mantra *japa* can be performed without willful effort. This practice can prepare you for *samādhi*.

Exercise 9-1

Mantra *Japa* without Willful Effort

Preparation:

Following the steps in Exercise 1-1, sit with proper posture, close your eyes, make a *sankalpa* to set aside your concerns, and perform the progressive relaxation exercise.

Practice – Part 1:

Begin silent recitation of a mantra of your choice. Give the mantra your full attention, letting it become firmly established in your mind. Continue with complete attention for ten minutes or more. When the mantra is well-established and your mind is completely free from wandering, proceed to Part 2.

Practice – Part 2:

Instead of willfully reciting the mantra, shift your perspective to become the observer or witness of your mind, as in the practice *Sākshī Bhāva* (Exercise 5-3). Separate and detach yourself from your mind so that you observe it as though from a distance. Observe the mantra being recited in your mind. Passively witness the flow of mantras, watching as they arise in the room of your mind and then fade away.

If your mind begins to wander, return to Part 1 and resume willful recitation of your mantra. When the mantra is once again well-established and your mind no longer wanders, continue with the practice of observing your mind as described in the previous paragraph.

Knowing the Knower

We now return to the second of the four categories of techniques, *observation*. Chapter Five introduced the practice of *sākshī bhāva* in which you observe the *vritti*s of your mind instead of trying to restrain them. By detaching yourself from your mind and observing its thoughts, perceptions, and emotions as though from a distance, you can passively witness the ever-changing flow of *vritti*s. A valuable new dimension of this technique will be introduced in this section.

In Chapter Five, a crucial principle was introduced — the distinction between *kshetra* and *kshetrajna*. *Kshetra* is the field of experience, all that is known. *Kshetrajna* is the knower, the knower of the field of experience. Here, we will explore the nature of the *kshetrajna*, the knower.

Patanjali provides an ideal starting point for this inquiry in the following *sutra*:

सदा ज्ञाताश्चित्तवृत्तयस्तत्प्रभोः पुरुषस्यापरिणामित्वात् ॥

sadā jnātāsh citta-vrittayas tat-prabhoh purushasyāparināmitvāt

Activities of the mind are always known
to the sovereign conscious being because it is unchanging.

YS 4.18

"Sovereign conscious being" refers to your essential awareful nature — the consciousness because of which you exist as a sentient being. You are aware of your thoughts, emotions, and perceptions. All these mental events are revealed by consciousness. They are illumined, as it were, like objects seen with the help of a flashlight. And the source of this illumination is your essential nature as a conscious being.

This discussion prepares us for the following question: Can consciousness itself be known in the same way that you know your thoughts and emotions? Examining this question more closely, it actually asks if consciousness can reveal consciousness. But such a query is like asking if a flashlight can illumine itself.

This tricky question is skillfully addressed in the Kena Upanishad:

यन्मनसा न मनुते येनाहुर्मनो मतम् ।

yan manasā na manute yenāhur mano matam

Wise ones say (consciousness) is
that which cannot be known by the mind
but that because of which the mind thinks.

KeU 1.6

"That because of which the mind thinks" refers to consciousness, the revealer of mental activities, the knower of all *vrittis*. Consciousness itself cannot be known because it is not a mental object; it is not a *vritti*. Rather, it is the awareful subject. It is you, the knower, the one whose consciousness illumines the activities of your mind.

This insight is followed by a remarkable declaration just a few verses later in the Kena Upanishad:

यस्यामतं तस्य मतं मतं यस्य न वदे सः ।

yasyāmatam tasya matam matam yasya na veda sah

For whom it is known, he does not know.
But for whom it is not known, he knows.

KeU 2.3

This is surely one of the most enigmatic statements to be found in any scripture. Yet it expresses a profound truth. The following paraphrase may help clarify its meaning:

One who (mistakenly) considers consciousness to be known (as an object) does not understand the nature of consciousness.

But one who understands that consciousness cannot be known (as an object) knows what consciousness truly is.

Consciousness is not a knowable object; it is the essence of you, the knower, the awareful subject. The very next verse of the *upanishad* explains that consciousness is *pratibodha-vidita*, known (*vidita*) in every experience (*pratibodha*). Consciousness is present in every moment and every experience as the light of awareness that reveals the activities of your mind.

Nature of Consciousness

Because consciousness is present in all our experiences, we generally consider it ordinary, nothing special. But when the true nature of consciousness is clearly recognized, it is discovered to be absolutely extraordinary. The *sutra* quoted earlier points to its extraordinary nature by saying that *vrittis* are known by consciousness "because it is unchanging."

Only an unchanging consciousness can allow you to witness your mind's constantly changing flow of thoughts, emotions, and perceptions. To illustrate this, imagine driving a car at sixty miles-per-hour and seeing someone drinking coffee while traveling in a car next to yours. That person would appear stationary to you. You could observe him drink coffee at sixty miles-per-hour only if you were standing motionless on the roadside. So too, only if your consciousness is unchanging can you accurately observe your fleeting thoughts, your shifting perceptions, and your evolving emotions. Your consciousness is an unwavering light of awareness that illumines the ever-changing activities of your mind.

To recognize that consciousness is unchanging is an insight with profound implications. To begin or end, to start or stop, to be born or to die—all these are changes. Since consciousness is unchanging, it cannot start or stop, so it must persist even while you are sound asleep. And since consciousness is unchanging, it cannot be born nor can it die, so it must precede your birth and survive the death of your body.

The *rishi*s discovered consciousness to be the divinity dwelling within us all, the true self, *ātmā*, which they described as *sat cit ānanda*. As explained in Chapter Two, *cit* means consciousness and *sat* means that which exists in the past, present, and future, that which exists without change. Thus consciousness is unborn, uncreated, and therefore eternal.

The word *ānanda* is usually translated as bliss, but it cannot mean a blissful feeling or ecstatic experience. *Sat cit ānanda* denotes the awareful experiencer, not something experienced. Scholarly commentaries on the *upanishad*s and other scriptures explain that *ānanda* is better understood as full, complete, boundaryless, and infinite.

How can you meditate on *sat cit ānanda*, on consciousness itself? Based on the above discussion, you cannot. *Ātmā* can never be an object of meditation because it is the awareful subject, it is the meditator's fundamental nature. Nevertheless, there are meditation techniques that can indeed help you appreciate the extraordinary nature of your consciousness as *sat cit ānanda.*

Ramana Maharshi was a great twentieth century teacher of Vedanta and a widely revered Hindu mystic. He advocated a simple but profound technique for discovering your true nature. He instructed followers to meditate and inquire "Who am I?" He taught that the ego or *ahankāra* can be traced back to its origin during meditation, and that its origin is pure consciousness, *sat cit ānanda.*

Ramana's method is actually a form of *contemplation.* As such, it belongs to the third category of meditation techniques. However, his method can fruitfully be combined with an *observation*-based technique — the practice of *sākshī bhāva.* The combination of *sākshī bhāva* and Ramana's "Who am I" inquiry can lead you to the core of your being, to the consciousness from which your ego arises, the consciousness that illumines all your thoughts. In this way, you can metaphorically meditate on the meditator by exploring, understanding, and appreciating your true nature as pure consciousness, as *sat cit ānanda.*

The following meditation exercise has two parts. The first part is *sākshī bhāva* as described in Exercise 5-3. It will help you detach from your mind and passively observe its activities as an awareful witness. The second part is based on Ramana's method of contemplation.

Exercise 9-2

Meditation on the Meditator

Preparation:

Sit with proper posture, close your eyes, and make a *sankalpa* to set aside your concerns as in Exercise 1-1. Instead of the progressive relaxation exercise, simply take several deep breaths to settle your mind.

Practice – Part 1:

Begin practicing *sākshī bhāva* as described in Exercise 5-3. First, observe sensations in each part of your body. Next, witness your breathing, tracing the passage of air and observing sensations at your nostrils. Finally, shift your perspective to separate and detach yourself from your mind and observe your mental activities as though from a distance. Imagine yourself sitting outside of the room of your mind, looking within and observing its contents. Take at least ten minutes to complete the above steps.

Practice – Part 2:

Reflect on the following questions, one at a time. Let your experience in *sākshī bhāva* and your understanding of *sat cit ānanda* guide your process of self-inquiry.

- Who is observing my mind?
- Am I my body, breath, or mind?
- Am I my thoughts, perceptions, or emotions?
- Who am I?
- Am I the consciousness by which all *vritti*s are known?
- Does this consciousness change?
- What is the nature of this consciousness?

Spend several minutes reflecting on each question. After finishing one question, resume your practice of *sākshī bhāva* for several minutes before proceeding to the next question.

Gap between Knowledge and Experience

In this section, we return to the third of our four basic categories of meditation techniques, *contemplation*. For techniques in this category, no effort is made to restrain thoughts or to observe them. Instead, specific kinds of thinking and reflection are employed to address important spiritual and emotional issues. One of those issues is the disparity or gap between knowledge and experience. This is a critical problem for all who follow the teachings of Vedanta. This gap is addressed by a form of contemplation known as *nididhyāsana* which is explained in this section.

An observation made by many students of Vedanta is, "I know that I am not my body or mind. I know that my true nature is *sat cit ānanda*. But I do not experience myself as *sat cit ānanda*. I still feel like an individual person with a body and mind." Here, the gap between knowledge and experience is apparent — they profess to *know* themselves as *sat cit ānanda* but they fail to *experience* themselves as such.

According to the teachings of Vedanta, the reason for this gap is the fact that experience often misleads us. We wrongly assume that knowledge and experience are always in perfect harmony. We are frequently deceived by many common experiences. These experiences seem to contradict what we already know to be true. For example, the sky appears blue, yet air is colorless. Objects seem solid, yet they are composed of atoms which are more than 99.999% empty space. We feel motionless when at rest, yet the earth is speeding around the sun at 67,000 miles-per-hour. Even simple optical illusions can deceive us.

A particularly helpful example of the gap between knowledge and experience is apparent whenever you gaze westward in the evening and watch the sun slowly set on the horizon. This familiar experience is surprisingly deceptive. The sun is actually stationary in the sky; it is the earth that moves, rotating on its axis. You *know* the sun does not travel through the sky. You *know* that sunset occurs because of the earth's rotation. But you still *experience* the sun going down each evening.

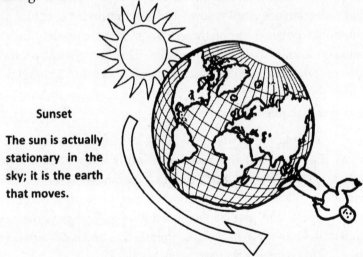

Sunset

The sun is actually stationary in the sky; it is the earth that moves.

This example demonstrates how easily we are misled by experience. Just as the sunset deceives us, we are deceived by the experience of our own bodies and minds. Even in the presence of clear, well-ascertained knowledge of ourselves as *sat cit ānanda*, the experience of our bodies and minds remains unchanged. We can *know* our true selves to be limitless and unchanging, yet still *experience* the limitations and vacillations of our bodies and minds. Thus a gap between knowledge and experience arises.

But we need not be deceived by such experiences; we can learn to interpret them properly. With regard to the sunset, our everyday experience tells us that huge things like buildings are stationary whereas smaller things like people and cars can move. So when the horizon appears vast compared to the sun, we naturally assume that the sun is going down rather than the horizon moving up. By understanding this properly, we can avoid being fooled by an optical illusion at sunset.

In the same way, we can learn how to properly interpret the experience of our own bodies and minds. We can learn that consciousness remains limitless and unchanging in spite of our limited and constantly changing experiences. Vedantic teachings can help us understand this well. In this way, we can learn to avoid being fooled by the experience of our own bodies and minds.

Nididhyāsana — Vedantic Contemplation

Even when we correctly interpret our experiences, the experiences themselves remain unchanged. The sun still appears to go down. We still experience the limitations of our bodies and minds. Thus a gap between knowledge and experience can persist in spite of our efforts to understand everything properly.

The gap between knowledge of *ātmā* and experience of our bodies and minds can be reconciled by Vedantic contemplation — *nididhyāsana*. To appreciate how *nididhyāsana* works, you could contemplate on the sunset. You could watch the sun go down while imagining yourself seated on a slowly rotating globe, gradually tilting over backwards. During this contemplation, the horizon would seem to move upwards towards the stationary sun. If you were to perform this contemplation for forty evenings in a row, you would no longer perceive the sun going down. You would think, "I am tipping over backwards."

The gap between your knowledge of earth's rotation and your experience of sunset can be closed by contemplation. In the same way, contemplation can close the gap between knowledge of yourself as *ātmā* and experience of your limited body and mind. This kind of contemplation is described in the meditation exercise at the end of this section.

Vedantic contemplation or *nididhyāsana* is the final step in a three-fold methodology that is the foundation upon which the teachings of Vedanta are based. The famous *rishi*, Yajnavalkya, explains this methodology to his wife, Maitreyi, in the following passage from the Brihadaranyaka Upanishad:

आत्मा वा अरे द्रष्टव्यः श्रोतव्यो मन्तव्यो निदिध्यासितव्यो मैत्रेयि ॥

ātmā vā are drashtavyah
shrotavyo mantavyo nididhyāsitavyo maitreyi

O Maitreyi, *ātmā* must be discovered. It must be inquired into, doubts must be removed, and it must be contemplated upon.

BrU 2.4.5

This important and well-known passage identifies the three basic practices of Vedanta:

Shravana—listening, a process of self-inquiry guided by the scriptures as heard from one's guru, culminating in the discovery of one's true nature, *ātmā*.

Manana—thinking or reflection, a process of removing any doubts or vagueness that could hinder one's self-knowledge.

Nididhyāsana—contemplation, a process of absorbing or assimilating the knowledge gained through *shravana* and rendered doubt-free through *manana*.

Vedantic practice begins with *shravana*, listening. But *shravana* is much more than merely hearing the teachings of Vedanta. These teachings must be carefully followed in a personal process of self-inquiry that leads you to discover *ātmā*. As the practice of *shravana* proceeds, doubts can arise and certain teachings can seem vague. For this reason, *shravana* is accompanied by *manana*, a process in which logical analysis and careful examination of Vedantic teachings are used to resolve doubts and remove any lack of clarity.

The last phase of Vedantic practice, *nididhyāsana*, closes the gap between knowledge and experience. In closing the gap, there are two main objectives. First, habitual identification with your body and mind must be removed. Second, knowledge of your true nature as *sat cit ānanda* must be thoroughly assimilated so that it completely transforms your thinking.

To understand the problem of habitual identification, consider the following. When an ordinary virus infects your body, you say, "I have a cold." You do not say, "My body has a cold." You regard yourself as your body, even though you know it is an object in which you dwell as a conscious being. In spite of this knowledge, you remain habitually identified with your body.

Similarly, when sadness fills your mind, you say, "I am sad." You never say, "Sadness is present in my mind." You habitually identify yourself with your mind in spite of understanding that thoughts and emotions are mental objects observed by you. Such confusion persists in spite of your knowledge, as it does for the sunset, due to the habitual nature of the mind.

Nididhyāsana can remove habitual identification with your body and mind by helping you develop an enduring appreciation of yourself as *sat cit ānanda* – unborn, changeless, thought-free consciousness. Deeply engrained wrong notions about yourself can be removed in meditation by repeatedly discerning yourself to be thought-free consciousness, independent of your body and mind. This practice of *nididhyāsana* works exactly the same way as the contemplation on the sunset described before.

The following meditation exercise introduces a form of *nididhyāsana* which can help you appreciate your true nature as thought-free consciousness. Such a recognition can be accomplished easily in the total absence of *vrittis*. When all thoughts, perceptions, and emotions have faded from your mind, thought-free consciousness alone remains. Therefore this form of *nididhyāsana* requires a completely silent mind.

To make your mind completely silent may seem like a daunting task. Fortunately, it is not difficult to silence your mind for just a few moments, and a few moments are all that is needed. It does not take long to recognize an old acquaintance, nor does it take long to recognize your true nature. A few moments are truly enough.

During mantra *japa*, there is a brief moment of silence between repetitions of the mantra. In that gap between mantras, no *vrittis* are present. And in that gap of silence, thought-free consciousness alone remains, available for recognition. As you meditate, you can gradually increase the length of the gap between mantras to provide a better opportunity for this recognition. In each interval of silence, you remain present as thought-free consciousness. After the moment of silence has passed, you can reflect on your experience in the gap. This reflection can allow you to verify or confirm your true nature as thought-free consciousness.

Exercise 9-3

Silence Between Mantras

Preparation:

Following the steps in Exercise 1-1, sit with proper posture, close your eyes, make a *sankalpa* to set aside your concerns, and perform the progressive relaxation exercise.

Practice – Part 1:

Begin silent recitation of a mantra of your choice. Give the mantra your full attention, letting it become firmly established in your mind. Continue with complete attention for ten minutes or more. When the mantra is well-established and your mind is completely free from wandering, proceed to Part 2.

Practice – Part 2:

Gradually lengthen the gap between mantras, allowing a longer interval of silence to separate them. If the gap becomes too long and your mind starts to wander, shorten the gap until your attention is once again completely focused on the mantra.

Practice – Part 3:

From time to time, stop reciting the mantra and reflect on your experience during the silence between mantras. Recognize your own presence in those gaps as thought-free consciousness. After reflecting on your experience of silence, resume recitation of the mantra as in Part 2.

Meditation on *Brahman*

In the final section of this chapter, we return to the last of our four categories of meditation techniques, *devotion*. The prior chapter introduced the devotional meditation practices of *upāsana*. There, various ways of meditating on Ishvara were described. This section introduces meditation on *brahman*, the fundamental reality because of which everything exists.

In Vedanta, Ishvara is also known as *saguna brahman*. *Saguna* means having qualities or attributes. *Saguna brahman* denotes Ishvara's many forms or aspects — as creator, giver of blessings, dispenser of karma, and so on. *Saguna brahman* was the focus of the meditation exercises in the previous chapter.

It is also possible to meditate on *nirguna brahman, brahman* without qualities, without form, without any attributes whatsoever. In the Mundaka Upanishad, *nirguna brahman* is described as:

यत्तद्द्रेश्यमग्राह्यमगोत्रमवर्णमचक्षुःश्रोत्रं तदपाणिपादं ।

yat tad adreshyam agrāhyam agotram avarnam
acakshuh-shrotram tad apāni-pādam

That (*brahman*) cannot be seen or grasped; it has
no origin, no qualities, no eyes or ears, no hands or feet.

MuU 1.1.6

But how can you meditate on something that has no form, no attributes or qualities, something unknown and inconceivable? My guru is fond of asking rhetorically, "How can you meditate on *gagabugai?*" *Gagabugai*, he explains, is a nonsense word he made up.

Because *nirguna brahman* has no form or attributes, it can never be an object of meditation. But its existence can indeed be known. *Nirguna brahman* can be recognized as the reality because of which everything exists. The *rishis* discovered this truth and expressed it in the second half of the verse quoted above:

नित्यं विभुं सर्वगतं सुसूक्ष्मं तद्व्ययं यद्भूतयोनिं परिपश्यन्ति धीराः ।

nityam vibhum sarvagatam susūkshmam tad avyayam
yad bhūta-yonim paripashyanti dhīrāh

Wise ones perceive everywhere the eternal, vast, all-pervasive, utterly formless, unchanging source of existence.

MuU 1.1.6

Nirguna brahman is the all-encompassing reality that gives existence to everything, including your body, your mind, your *vrittis*, and even your consciousness. *Nirguna brahman* is not a distant, imperceptible object. It is your own true self, *ātmā*. This is indeed the highest truth of Vedanta which the *rishis* expressed in declarations called *mahāvākyas*, such as *tat tvam asi* – you are that, *prajnānam brahma* – consciousness is *brahman*, and *aham brahmāsmi* – I am *brahman*.

Because *nirguna brahman* is immediately present as the reality because of which you exist, it can be appreciated in meditation, not as an object, but as your true self, as *sat cit ānanda*. *Nirguna brahman* can be known as the pure consciousness which remains in the absence of thoughts, perceptions, and emotions. In the perfect silence attained in deep meditation, all that remains is the reality of yourself, the reality of all — *nirguna brahman.*

In his *sutras*, Patanjali prescribes a technique for meditating on *brahman*. Since *nirguna brahman* can never become an object of meditation, the method Patanjali provides is for meditating on *saguna brahman*:

तस्य वाचकः प्रणवः ॥ तज्जपस्तदर्थभावनम् ॥

tasya vācakah pranavah | taj-japas tad-artha-bhāvanam

Om is name for that (Ishvara, *saguna brahman*).
Repeat it and contemplate its meaning.

YS 1.27-28

Om is a one-syllable mantra, a sound-symbol that represents Ishvara, *saguna brahman*. In this *sutra*, Patanjali prescribes not only recitation of *om*, but also contemplation on its meaning.

The meaning of *om* is symbolically hidden in the mantra itself. The letter *o* is a diphthong or complex vowel. It is grammatically considered a combination of the letters *a* and *u*. Therefore *om* can be expanded into three letters: *a-u-m*. Please note that this expansion is for symbolic reasons only. In Sanskrit, it is entirely incorrect for *om* to be written or pronounced as *aum*.

The symbolism of *a-u-m* can be interpreted in several ways. With regard to *saguna brahman*, the letter *a* represents Ishvara as creator of the universe. The letter *u* represents Ishvara as the power that sustains the universe. And the letter *m* represents Ishvara as the one unto whom the universe returns at the end of time. From a mythological standpoint, these three letters represent Brahma, Vishnu, and Shiva — God as creator, sustainer, and destroyer. This three-fold symbolism makes *om* ideal for meditation on *saguna brahman*.

Om can also be used in meditation to appreciate the existence of *nirguna brahman*. While reciting *om*, a small gap or moment of silence occurs between repetitions, as discussed before. In that silence, consciousness alone remains. And that consciousness is non-different from *nirguna brahman*, as the *rishis* revealed in the *mahāvākyas* quoted earlier.

Whereas *saguna brahman* can be symbolically represented by the mantra *om*, *nirguna brahman*, which has no qualities or attributes, cannot be represented by any mantra, sound, form, or symbol. Silence alone can truly represent *nirguna brahman*. And that silence can be appreciated in meditation, especially in the gap between repetitions of *om*.

The following meditation exercise introduces a form of *upāsana* or meditation on *brahman* known as *brahmopāsana*. It is based on recitation of the mantra *om*. During each repetition of *om*, you can meditate on *saguna brahman* by reflecting on the three-fold symbolism of *a-u-m* representing Ishvara as creator, sustainer, and destroyer. In the gap between mantras, during the moment of silence when thought-free consciousness alone remains, you can appreciate the existence of the attribute-free absolute reality, *nirguna brahman*.

Exercise 9-4

Meditation on *Brahman – Brahmopāsana*

Preparation:

Following the steps in Exercise 1-1, sit with proper posture, close your eyes, make a *sankalpa* to set aside your concerns, and perform the progressive relaxation exercise.

Practice – Part 1:

Begin silent recitation of *om*. Give the mantra your full attention, letting it become firmly established in your mind. Continue with complete attention for ten minutes or more. When the mantra is well-established and your mind is free from wandering, proceed to Part 2.

Practice – Part 2:

Gradually lengthen the gap between mantras, allowing a longer interval of silence to separate them. If the gap becomes too long and your mind starts to wander, shorten the gap until your attention is once again completely focused on the mantra.

Practice – Part 3:

From time to time, stop reciting *om* and reflect on its meaning as *saguna brahman*—Ishvara as the source, sustainer, and ultimate end of the world.

Reflect also on the gap between mantras, the moment of silence when thought-free consciousness alone remains. Reflect on the *rishis'* revelation that consciousness is non-different from *nirguna brahman*, the attribute-free absolute reality because of which everything exists.

After contemplating on *om* and the gap between mantras for a few minutes, resume recitation of *om* as in Parts 1 and 2. Repeat this sequence.

CHAPTER TEN

DEVELOPING YOUR PRACTICE

We have come to the last chapter of this book which is dedicated to providing guidance for your ongoing practice of meditation. In the very first chapter, meditation was described as a learned skill. It takes time to learn to meditate. To further develop your skills and build a powerful, highly-refined practice, even more time and effort is required.

If you were learning a musical instrument, it could take months or years to thoroughly master the basics. And to perform at a professional level, even more practice would be required. But you could never reach that level without first mastering the basics and building a firm foundation. For meditation, building a firm foundation is equally essential. And there is only one way to accomplish this: meditate.

The requirements for building a firm foundation are described by Patanjali in the following *sutra*:

स तु दीर्घकालनैरन्तर्यसत्कारासेवितो दृढभूमिः ॥

sa tu dīrgha-kāla-nairantarya-satkārāsevito dridha-bhūmih

That (practice) builds a firm foundation
when done properly for a long time without interruption.

YS 1.14

There is no secret formula or special trick for building a firm foundation. As mentioned in the first chapter, it is a matter of daily practice. The more you meditate, the stronger your foundation will become. With ongoing effort, progress is inevitable, but it requires time and patience.

Developing your skills is a natural process. It occurs slowly and steadily, like the growth of a plant. Plants do not grow overnight, nor does your ability to meditate. But as long as a plant receives water and light, it grows taller. And as long as your practice receives time and effort, it grows stronger.

In the Bhagavad Gita, Sri Krishna teaches that persistent, ongoing effort is necessary:

शनैः शनैरुपरमेद् बुद्ध्या धृतिगृहीतया ।

shanaih shanair uparamed buddhyā dhriti-grihītayā

With a determined intellect, quiet (your mind) gradually.

BG 6.25

Sometimes, progress does not come as quickly as we want or expect. This is more often due to having unreasonable expectations than to actual lack of progress. If you were to watch a plant for hours on end, waiting for it to grow taller, you would not see any growth whatsoever. In the same way, you might not perceive any improvement in your meditation from one day to the next.

Some meditators have a complaint similar to that of many musicians. After months of intense practice, musicians might not hear any improvement in their performance, even though listeners praise them for making great strides. Why can't the musicians hear their own progress? As their talent grows, their expectations grow as well, even to the extent that they feel like they have made no progress at all.

The same thing happens for many meditators. As your skills improve, your expectations can grow higher, leading you to feel like you are not making any progress. But such feelings are deceptive. If you understand the nature of expectations, you can avoid frustration and disappointment. You can drop your expectations knowing that progress is certain as long as you keep practicing.

Overcoming Obstacles to Progress

There are many obstacles that can hinder efforts to improve the quality and depth of meditation. Some obstacles are due to the natural limitations of our bodies and minds. Others are inadvertently created by ourselves. For example, some meditators impatiently move on to advanced techniques before mastering the basics. But the process of learning cannot be rushed, just as a plant's growth cannot be rushed. Impatience can be a huge obstacle for meditators.

Impatience can also lead to skipping the necessary steps of preparation before each session. In Exercise 1-1, three basic preliminary steps were described — sitting with proper posture, making a *sankalpa* to set aside concerns, and a progressive relaxation exercise. Without proper preparation, successful practice of any meditation technique can be hampered.

Preparation is crucial. Musicians must tune their instruments or warm their voices before performing. Cooks must clean and cut the vegetables before putting them into a pot. Without adequate preparation, musicians will perform badly and cooks will prepare tasteless dishes. Taking short cuts may save a few minutes, but lack of proper preparation leads to failure in the long run.

The aforementioned three steps—*āsana*, *sankalpa*, and relaxation—can be considered the minimum requirements for preparing to meditate. Sometimes, additional preparation is required. If you continually struggle to quiet your mind, you might need to include a fourth step of preparation—the practice of *prānāyāma*, breathing exercises.

Patanjali prescribes that *prānāyāma* should be practiced before proceeding to the following limbs of yoga: *pratyāhāra*, *dhāranā* and *dhyāna*. In Chapter Two, several important breathing techniques were introduced, including *Nādi Shodhana*, Slow Deep Breathing, and *Ujjayī Prānāyāma* (Exercises 2-2, 2-3, and 2-4). Any of these could be included after the three basic steps of preparation. This additional step might be indispensible for some meditators.

In addition to impatience and inadequate preparation, many other obstacles can get in the way of developing your practice. Patanjali lists no fewer than nine such obstacles in the following *sutra*:

व्याधिस्त्यानसंशयप्रमादालस्याविरतिभ्रान्तिदर्शनालब्ध -
भूमिकत्वानवस्थितत्वानि चित्तविक्षेपास्तेऽन्तरायाः ॥

vyādhi-styāna-samshaya-pramādālasyāvirati-bhrānti-darshanālabdha-
bhūmikatvānavasthitatvāni citta-vikshepās te 'ntarāyāh

YS 1.30

The obstacles that affect the mind are:

Vyādhi – physical illness. Lack of sufficient strength and stamina to support intense meditation practice.

Styāna – distractedness. Inability to focus or concentrate your attention, preoccupation with worldly things and activities.

Samshaya – doubt. Uncertainty, lack of clarity about spiritual teachings due to inadequate study or improper guidance.

Pramāda – carelessness. Inattention, lack of commitment, failure to establish a regular routine of meditation.

Ālasyā – lethargy. Drowsiness, dullness, lack of mental energy.

Avirati – lack of detachment. Strong attraction to worldly things and activities, sensuality.

Bhrānti-darshana – misconception. Holding wrong conclusions, false assumptions, or incorrect interpretations of scripture.

Alabdha-bhūmikatva – absence of foundation. Failure to master the basics of meditation and build a firm base for practice.

Anavasthitatva – instability. Inability to sustain effort for a sufficient length of time, lack of tenacity, impatience.

Any of these obstacles can hinder your efforts to build a strong meditation practice. Fortunately, all these can be overcome if they are recognized and appropriate steps are taken to overcome them.

Sri Krishna speaks of the need to overcome several other obstacles in the following verse from the Bhagavad Gita:

युक्ताहारविहारस्य युक्तचेष्टस्य कर्मसु ।
युक्तस्वप्नावबोधस्य योगो भवति दुःखहा ॥

yuktāhāra-vihārasya yukta-ceshtasya karmasu
yukta-svapnāvabodhasya yogo bhavati duhkhahā

Meditation removes suffering for one whose diet,
recreation, work, and sleep are balanced.

BG 6.17

This verse addresses the need to overcome obstacles related to lifestyle—diet, recreation, work, and sleep. A stressful, unhealthy lifestyle with poor diet, excessive work, no leisure, and insufficient sleep can not only ruin your meditation practice, but it can harm your body and mind. Such issues cannot be ignored. It might be helpful to examine your own lifestyle to see what needs attention.

Becoming drowsy or falling asleep during meditation are problems I often hear from my students. When I ask them how much sleep they get each night, the answer is usually six hours or less. But many people need seven, eight, or more hours of sleep to feel fully rested. Unfortunately, few manage to get as much sleep as their bodies truly need. It is interesting to note that before the advent of electric lighting just one-hundred years ago, the average length of a night's sleep was ten hours.

Some medical researchers have suggested that our country suffers from an epidemic of sleep deprivation. They found that the effects of not sleeping enough each night is cumulative. Over four or five nights, you can accrue a large sleep deficit that significantly diminishes your alertness, attention span, and ability to concentrate. Ironically, sleep is often cut short to accomplish more each day, but if you are less efficient due to sleep deprivation, you might actually accomplish less. With an extra hour of sleep each night, you can be more energetic throughout the day, more efficient in your work, and more alert for meditation.

Here are some other suggestions for avoiding drowsiness during meditation. Sit on a thin cushion or firm chair with your spine erect and your shoulders thrown back to open up your chest. Sitting on an overstuffed chair or plump cushion can promote drowsiness, as can a lazy, slumping posture. Cool, fresh air can also help you stay alert. Open a window and put on extra clothing if necessary to stay warm.

Finally, if you drink tea or coffee, you might find it helpful to have a cup before meditating. Some may object to this suggestion, based on scriptural prohibitions against the use of intoxicants. But those texts actually refer to substances that dull the mind like alcohol and certain drugs. Tea and coffee, on the other hand, are mild stimulants that can improve your alertness. On the other hand, if you struggle with restlessness rather than drowsiness during meditation, you should certainly avoid tea and coffee.

Practice — Regular and Sustained

As discussed in Chapter One, regular meditation is essential. Not surprisingly, the benefits of meditation depend entirely on how much effort you put into your practice. To meditate once a week or less will yield very modest results. But daily practice, when sustained over a period of months and years, can produce remarkable benefits.

Consistent, long-term practice of techniques from each of the four basic categories of meditation can produce extraordinary benefits such as:

Concentration: These techniques can lead you to discover a vast inner space that is profoundly silent, timeless, and limitless, a space in which your consciousness shines unobstructed by mental events while imparting contentment, fullness, and perfect peace.

Observation: These techniques can help you become completely detached from your body, mind, and the world around you, giving you tremendous inner freedom and profound insight into the subtle workings of your mind.

Contemplation: These techniques can free you from anger, hurt, resentment, and dysfunctional patterns of thinking while engendering gratitude, acceptance, and great clarity about your true nature.

Devotion: These techniques can lead you to discover Ishvara's presence, both within you and around you, fostering a deep sense of reverence and intimacy in which you feel emotionally connected to God at all times.

The above-mentioned results are not the rare achievements of a few gifted meditators. Anyone can attain them, but only with *regular* and *sustained* practice. This is the key to experiencing profoundly rewarding meditations.

The Shvetashvatara Upanishad stresses the importance of both regular and sustained practice in two different passages. Sustained practice is considered in the following verse that compares meditation to starting a fire by rubbing two pieces of wood together:

स्वदेहमरणिं कृत्वा प्रणवं चोत्तरारणिम् ।
ध्याननिर्मथनाभ्यासादेवं पश्येन्निगूढवत् ॥

svadeham aranim kritvā pranavam cottarāranim
dhyāna-nirmathanābhyāsād devam pashyen nigūdhavat

Make your body the lower stick and make *om* the upper.
By the constant rubbing of meditation,
discover the light hidden within.

ShvU 1.14

In ancient India's pre-scientific culture, fire was thought to be hidden in wood, waiting to be coaxed out by vigorously rubbing two pieces of wood together. This verse presents a powerful metaphor—just as fire is hidden in wood, *ātmā* is hidden in yourself. And just as vigorous rubbing can reveal the fire, so too, extensive recitation of *om* (or any mantra) can reveal the presence of *ātmā*.

If you rub two sticks together, heat builds up gradually due to friction. You have to rub vigorously for a long time to generate enough heat to start a fire. If you stop before fire is produced, the sticks will cool immediately and you will have to start over. Sustained effort is the key to starting a fire. In the same way, sustained effort is the key to advancing to deeper levels of meditation. Intense, sustained practice can hasten the Vedantic process of self-inquiry and help ignite the fire of wisdom, *jnānāgni*, that can burn away ignorance and lead to enlightenment.

Having considered the importance of *sustained* practice, we can now discuss the importance of *regular* practice. Igniting the fire of wisdom is a long-term goal. This process may go on for months, years, or even decades. Yet there are many immediate benefits of meditation that can be reaped from each day's practice. For example, meditation can calm your mind while removing agitation, frustration, resentment, and the like. As discussed in Chapter 7, meditation can produce *antahkarana shuddhi*, purity of mind. Meditation can help cleanse your mind of all that is undesirable.

The Shvetashvatara Upanishad presents a beautiful analogy in which your mind is compared to a mirror:

यथैव बिम्बं मृदयोपलिप्तं तेजोमयं भ्राजते तत्सुधान्तम् ।
yathaiva bimbam mridayopaliptam tejomayam bhrājate tat sudhāntam

(Mind is) like a dirty mirror that shines brightly when cleaned.
ShvU 2.14

To expand on this metaphor, when your mind is free from agitation, frustration, and resentment, it can vividly reflect the divinity within you. Then you will shine with peace, contentment, and kindness. But when your mind is sullied with emotional impurities, few can see the divinity within you. It is obstructed from view because the mirror of your mind is too dirty to reflect it. Fortunately, your mind-mirror is easily cleansed by meditation.

Every mirror, like the one in your bathroom, requires regular cleaning. The mirror of your mind is no different. Every day, your mind picks up numerous impurities—all the hurts, irritations, and frustrations that naturally occur with the activities of life. Anything used in an activity becomes dirty and requires cleaning. You wash dishes after a meal and you wash your clothes after wearing them all day. In the same way, the mirror of your mind must be cleansed of impurities acquired from its activities. And since your mind gets soiled every day, it requires daily purification. Daily meditation is needed to cleanse the mirror of your mind so that it can reflect the divinity within you as brightly as possible.

Experimentation and Exploration

Over time, some meditators gradually lose their enthusiasm for practice. Their favorite techniques might slowly become monotonous. Then, if each session seems repetitive and no progress is seen, their commitment to ongoing practice could wane. If they eventually lose their interest and value for meditation, they might give up their practice altogether, which would be a great loss.

The key to maintaining your enthusiasm for meditation is to avoid a static, boring routine. It is extremely helpful to develop a practice that constantly evolves, a practice in which each session leads you a little further along the path of spiritual growth. To create an effective, compelling practice is not difficult if you cultivate two crucial qualities — the attitude of *experimentation* and the attitude of *exploration*.

The attitude of *experimentation* can lead you to try out new techniques instead of rigidly holding on to a tiresome, long-standing routine. A technique you once found very powerful could gradually lose its effectiveness. Such experiences are not uncommon. Your willingness to let go of familiar, lackluster techniques and seek out new, more effective ones can help you build a strong, thriving practice.

In addition to trying new techniques, you can experiment by combining techniques in various ways. In a single session, you can practice two or three different techniques, one after another. You can also modify techniques to suit your own preferences. The procedures described in each exercise of this book are not sacrosanct rituals that must be followed without alteration. You can adapt them in any way that seems beneficial.

For this process of experimentation, you need not depend on outside guidance. After all, you alone know what works best to quiet your mind and focus your attention. Therefore, your common sense is the best source of guidance. Any technique that works well is worth using again; those that do not work can be set aside. There is no right way or wrong way to meditate. As explained in the introduction, everyone responds differently to various techniques. You must discover what works best for you.

With regard to experimenting with various techniques, the following warning is sometimes raised: You cannot find water by digging many shallow holes in different places; you must choose one place and dig deep. This proverb suggests that it is better to choose one technique and stick with it rather than trying others. This proverb conveys some genuine wisdom, but it has a critical shortcoming. Specifically, what happens if you are digging in the wrong place?

If there is no water below, all efforts to dig deep will be wasted. In the same way, if a particular meditation technique does not help quiet your mind and focus your attention, to continue using it can be a waste of time. Before digging a deep well, it is desirable to find the best place to dig. And before plunging deeply into the practice of meditation, it is desirable to experiment with a variety of techniques to find those which are most effective.

The second of the two attitudes mentioned before, *exploration*, is equally important for building and sustaining your practice. As noted before, different kinds of meditation have differing purposes and results. The wide range of exercises provided in this book is intended to support your own exploration of various dimensions of meditation and spiritual growth. This exploration is actually an inquiry into your own self. It is a journey within to explore the same inner realms surveyed by the *rishis* so long ago.

Meditation can be a life-long journey of exploration. After more than thirty years, I continue to learn and grow from each day's practice. No two of my meditation sessions are alike. Each morning I sit with a sense of anticipation, eager to discover new insights. To me, meditation is like a journey through a beautiful countryside, traversing craggy mountains and deep valleys strewn with colorful flowers. I always feel excited to climb the next peak to see what lies in the valley beyond.

A vast spiritual landscape exists within you, waiting to be explored. Along its paths, you can behold realms of astonishing beauty and discover treasures of great value, all hidden far from ordinary worldly life. Experiences like these can transform your life.

Yet meditation is more than an exploration of the *breadth* of this extraordinary inner terrain; it is also an exploration of its *depth*. Over time, you can learn to lead your mind to a place of profound silence. You can develop the capacity for laser-like concentration and the ability to remain deeply absorbed for extended periods of time.

With such skills, you can dive deep, piercing layer after layer of thoughts, perceptions, and emotions. Eventually, you can reach the core of your being, your true self, *ātmā*. And when you arrive, you will have the opportunity to personally discover what the ancient *rishi*s discovered — that the seeker is the sought, that you have always been *sat cit ānanda*, uncreated, limitless consciousness, and that Ishvara has always been present, bestowing infinite blessings upon you.

MANTRAS FOR MEDITATION

This appendix provides a selection of commonly used mantras together with explanations of their meanings. Less-common mantras, tantric mantras, and mantras requiring personal initiation from a guru have not been included.

Mantras should be pronounced correctly, whether they are recited aloud or silently. Vedic mantras usually have *svaras* or pitches associated with each syllable; these should be properly intoned. Audio recordings that demonstrate proper pronunciation and intonation of each mantra in this appendix can be found on our ashram's website. Please see the online resources listed in Appendix B for further details.

This appendix also includes meditation verses (*dhyāna shlokas*) for a number of deities, along with word by word translations and brief explanations of the symbolism associated with those deities. In the word for word translations, spelling changes due to grammar rules have been corrected and word order has been adjusted to improve clarity and readability.

Pranava Mantra — *Om*

Pranava is the Sanskrit name for *om*, a sound-symbol that represents Ishvara. It is included as an invocation at the beginning of most mantras.

As explained in Chapter 9, *om* can be grammatically deconstructed into *a–u–m* for symbolic purposes, though it should never be written or pronounced as *aum*. There are two main interpretations of these three letters. They can represent the creator, sustainer, and destroyer of the universe — Brahma, Vishnu, and Shiva — respectively. Or according to the Mandukya Upanishad, they can represent the three states of experience: *a* = waking state, *u* = dream state, and *m* = deep sleep state. The gap of silence between repetitions of *om* represents the consciousness from which *om* arises and into which it resolves.

Bīja Mantras — Seed Syllables

Bīja mantras are also sound-symbols like *om*. Because they are one syllable long, they are also called *bījāksharas*, seed (*bīja*) syllables (*akshara*). *Om* itself is a *bījākshara*.

Bīja mantras are usually associated with a particular deity, though these connections vary somewhat. Shown below is a list of common *bīja* mantras and the deities with which they are most commonly associated:

ॐ	*om*	*Pranava* — invokes Ishvara.
गं	*gam*	*Ganapati bīja* — invokes Ganesha.
दुं	*dum*	*Durgā bīja* — invokes Durga.

ऐं	aim	*Sarasvati bīja* — invokes Sarasvati.
श्रीं	shrīm	*Lakshmī bīja* — invokes Lakshmi.
ह्रीं	hrīm	*Lajja bīja* — invokes Parvati.
क्रीं	krīm	*Kālī bīja* — invokes Kali.
क्लीं	klīm	*Kāma bīja* — invokes various deities.

Mantras for Beginners

This appendix contains a fairly extensive compilation of mantras. If you are a beginning meditator selecting a mantra for the first time, you might find yourself bewildered by the bulkiness of this information. To simplify the process of choosing a mantra, a selection of the most commonly used mantras is provided below. You can return to this appendix at any time to browse through all the other mantras included.

Mantra for Ganesha

ॐ गं गणपतये नमः ॥

om gam ganapataye namah
Om! Salutations to Ganapati.

gam—invocation of Ganesha, *ganapataye*—to Ganesha or Ganapati, the master (*pati*) of Shiva's retinue (*gana*), *namah*—salutations.

Mantra for Vishnu

ॐ नमो नारायणाय ॥

om namo nārāyanāya

Om! Salutations to Narayana.

namah—salutations, *nārāyanāya*—to Narayana or Vishnu.

Mantra for Krishna

ॐ नमो भगवते वासुदेवाय ॥

om namo bhagavate vāsudevāya

Om! Salutations to Bhagavan Sri Krishna.

namah—salutations, *bhagavate*—to Bhagavan, *vāsudevāya*—to the son of Vasudeva, Sri Krishna.

Mantra for Rama

ॐ श्रीराम जय राम जय जय राम ॥

om shrī-rām jay rām jay jay rām

Om! Hail Rama.

shrī—term of respect, *rām*—O Rama, *jay*—hail.

Mantra for Shiva

ॐ नमः शिवाय ॥

om namah shivāya

Om! Salutations to Shiva.

namah—salutations, *shivāya*—to Shiva.

Mantra for Sarasvati

ॐ ऐं सरस्वत्यै नमः ॥

om aim sarasvatyai namah
Om! Salutations to Sarasvati.

aim—invocation of Sarasvati, *sarasvatyai*—to Sarasvati, *namah*—salutations.

Gayatri Mantra

The Gayatri Mantra is not addressed to goddess Gayatri, as some might think. It is addressed to Surya, God as the sun, who is called Savita in this mantra. The mantra's name is derived from the poetic meter in which it is composed — *gāyatrī cchandas.* There are other mantras in the *gāyatrī* meter addressed to deities like Vishnu and Shiva. Some of these are included later in this appendix.

The Gayatri Mantra is from the Rig Veda. It has probably been chanted more widely than any other mantra. Symbolically, Savita or God in the form of the sun represents Ishvara as the source of all knowledge, especially as the source of spiritual wisdom. Therefore, this mantra is a prayer for the light of spiritual wisdom, for enlightenment.

Gayatri Mantra

ॐ भूर्भुवस्स्वः ॥
तत्सवितुर्वरेण्यं भर्गो देवस्य धीमहि । धियो यो नः प्रचोदयात् ॥

om bhūr bhuvas svah
tat savitur varenyam bhargo devasya dhīmahi
dhiyo yo nah pracodayāt

Om! God of earth, sky, and heavens!
We meditate on the divine light of God as the sun.
May He guide our minds.

bhūh bhuvah svah—invocation of Ishvara on earth, in the sky, and in the heavens respectively; *dhīmahi*—we meditate, *tat*—on that, *varenyam*—divine, *bhargas*—light, *devasya*—of God, *savituh*—of Savita, God as the sun; *yah*—He, *pracodayāt*—may He guide, *nah*—our, *dhiyah*—minds.

Mantras for Ganesha

Ganesha is a form of Ishvara that represents God's capacity to remove obstacles from our lives. Depictions vary widely, but Ganesha is most commonly shown with four arms. His upper right hand holds an axe, *parashu*, used to remove obstacles. His upper left hand holds a snare, *pāsha*, used to gather His devotees. His lower right hand is held in *abhaya*

234

mudra, a gesture assuring there is nothing to fear. Or it may hold the broken tusk used to write out the Mahabharata. His lower left hand holds a *modaka,* a sweet representing His blessings.

His elephant head represents intelligence and his large stomach symbolically contains all the worlds. His vehicle is a mouse, *mushaka,* representing the force of desire which is always under Ganesha's control.

Meditation Verse for Ganesha — *dhyāna shloka*

वक्रतुण्ड महाकाय सूर्यकोटिसमप्रभ ।
निर्विघ्नं कुरु मे देव सर्वकार्येषु सर्वदा ॥

vakra-tunda mahākāya sūrya-koti-samaprabha
nirvighnam kuru me deva sarva-kāryeshu sarvadā

O God (*deva*) with a curved (*vakra*) trunk (*tunda*) and huge (*mahā*) body (*kāya*), shining like (*sama-prabha*) millions (*koti*) of suns (*sūrya*). Grant (*kuru*) me (*me*) freedom from obstacles (*nirvighna*), in all (*sarva*) endeavors (*kārya*), always (*sarvadā*).

Ganesha Mantra

ॐ श्रीगणेशाय नमः ॥

om shrī-ganeshāya namah
Om! Salutations to Ganesha.

shrī—term of respect, *ganeshāya*—to Ganesha, the master (*īsha*) of Shiva's retinue (*gana*), *namah*—salutations.

Mahaganapati Mantra

ॐ श्रीमहागणपतये नमः ॥

om shrī-mahāganapataye namah
Om! Salutations to Mahaganapati.

shrī—term of respect, *mahāganapataye*—to Mahaganapati, the great (*mahā*) master (*pati*) of Shiva's retinue (*gana*), *namah*—salutations.

Ganapati Mula Mantra

ॐ गं गणपतये नमः ॥

om gam ganapataye namah
Om! Salutations to Ganapati

gam—invocation of Ganesha, *ganapataye*—to Ganapati, the master (*pati*) of Shiva's retinue (*gana*), *namah*—salutations.

Ganapati Gayatri

ॐ एकदन्ताय विद्महे वक्रतुण्डाय धीमहि ।
तन्नो दन्तिः प्रचोदयात् ॥

om eka-dantāya vidmahe vakra-tundāya dhīmahi
tan no dantih pracodayāt

We contemplate (*vidmahe*) upon Him who has one (*eka*) tusk (*danta*). We meditate (*dhīmahi*) on Him who has a curved (*vakra*) trunk (*tunda*). Him (*tat*) with a tusk (*danti*), may He guide (*pracodayāt*) us (*nah*).

Mantras for Vishnu

Vishnu is a form of Ishvara representing God's power to sustain and preserve the universe. His dark color represents the infinite night sky. His upper right hand holds a discus, *chakra*, a symbol of power. His upper left hand holds a conch, *shankha*, symbolizing his blessings. His lower hands hold a mace, *gada*, symbol of protection, and a lotus, *padma*, which represents His consort, Lakshmi.

Meditation Verse for Vishnu — *dhyāna shloka*

शान्ताकारं भुजगशयनं पद्मनाभं सुरेशं
विश्वाधारं गगनसदृशं मेघवर्णं शुभाङ्गम् ।
लक्ष्मीकान्तं कमलनयनं योगिभिर्ध्यानगम्यं
वन्दे विष्णुं भवभयहरं सर्वलोकैकनाथम् ॥

shāntākāram bhūjaga-shayanam padma-nābham suresham
vishvādhāram gagana-sadrisham megha-varnam shubhāngam
lakshmī-kāntam kamala-nayanam yogibhir dhyāna-gamyam
vande vishnum bhava-bhaya-haram sarva-lokaikanātham

I worship (*vande*) Vishnu whose form (*ākāra*) is peaceful (*shānta*), reclining (*shayana*) on a serpent (*bhūjaga*), from whose navel (*nābhi*) rises a lotus flower (*padma*), Lord (*īsha*) of gods (*sura*), sustaining (*ādhāra*) the world (*vishva*), all-pervasive like (*sadrisha*) space

237

(*gagana*), whose complexion (*varna*) is like a dark cloud (*megha*), whose limbs (*anga*) are beautiful (*shubha*), loved (*kānta*) by goddess Lakshmi, lotus (*kamala*) eyed (*nayana*), attained (*gamya*) through meditation (*dhyāna*) by yogis (*yogibhih*), remover (*hara*) of worldly (*bhava*) fear (*bhaya*), the one (*eka*) Lord (*nātha*) of the world (*loka*).

Narayana Mantra

ॐ नमो नारायणाय ॥

om namo nārāyanāya

Om! Salutations to Narayana.

namah—salutations, *nārāyanāya*—to Narayana or Vishnu.

Vishnu Mantra

ॐ नमो विष्णवे प्रभविष्णवे ॥

om namo vishnave prabhavishnave

Om! Salutations to the effulgent Vishnu.

namah—salutations, *vishnave*—to Vishnu, *prabhavishnave*—to the effulgent one.

Venkateshvara Mantra

ॐ नमो वेङ्कटेशाय ॥

om namo venkateshāya

Om! Salutations to Venkateshvara.

namah—salutations, *venkateshāya*—to Venkatesha or Venkateshvara, Lord (*īsha*) of the mountain (*venkata*).

Vishnu Gayatri

ॐ नारायणाय विद्महे वासुदेवाय धीमहि ।
तन्नो विष्णुः प्रचोदयात् ॥

om nārāyanāya vidmahe vāsudevāya dhīmahi
tan no vishnuh prachodayāt

We contemplate (*vidmahe*) Narayana (*nārāyanāya*), we meditate (*dhīmahi*) on the son of Vasudeva, Krishna, (*vāsudevāya*). That (*tat*) Vishnu (vishnuh), may He guide (prachodayāt) us (nah).

Mantras for Krishna

The name Krishna means one who is very attractive. His flute and curved posture represent Ishvara's power to attract us emotionally. Krishna's dark color identifies him as an incarnation of Vishnu.

Meditation Verse for Krishna — *dhyāna shloka*

वसुदेवसुतं देवं कम्सचाणूरमर्दनम् ।
देवकीपरमानन्दं कृष्णं वन्दे जगद्गुरुम् ॥

vasudeva-sutam devam kamsa-cānūra-mardanam
devakī-paramānandam krishnam vande jagad-gurum

I worship (*vande*) the son (*suta*) of Vasudeva, the destroyer (*mardana*) of Kamsa and Chanura, the great joy (*paramānanda*) of Devaki, and the guru of the world (*jagad*).

Krishna Mantra

ॐ श्रीकृष्णाय नमः ॥

om shrī-krishnāya namah

Om! Salutations to Krishna.

shrī—term of respect, *krishnāya*—to Krishna, *namah*—salutations.

Krishna Mula Mantra

ॐ क्लीं कृष्णाय नमः ॥

om klīm krishnāya namah

Om! Klim! Salutations to Krishna.

klīm—invocation of Krishna, *krishnāya*—to Krishna, *namah*—salutations.

Vasudeva Mantra

ॐ नमो भगवते वासुदेवाय ॥

om namo bhagavate vāsudevāya

Om! Salutations to Bhagavan Krishna.

namah—salutations, *bhagavate*—to Bhagavan, *vāsudevāya*—to the son of Vasudeva, Krishna.

Krishna Sharana Mantra

ॐ श्रीकृष्णः शरणं मम ॥

om shrī-krishnah sharanam mama
Om! Krishna is my refuge.

shrī—term of respect, *krishnah*—Krishna, *mama*—my, *sharanam* —refuge.

Mahamantra

हरे कृष्ण हरे कृष्ण कृष्ण कृष्ण हरे हरे ।
हरे राम हरे राम राम राम हरे हरे ॥

hare krishna hare krishna krishna krishna hare hare
hare rāma hare rāma rāma rāma hare hare

hare—O Hari, *krishna*—O Krishna, *rāma*—O Rama.

Krishna Govinda Mantra

ॐ श्रीकृष्णाय गोविन्दाय गोपीजनवल्लभाय नमः ॥

om shrī-krishnāya govindāya gopījana-vallabhāya namah
Om! Salutations to Krishna, the cowherd loved by the *gopis*.

shrī—term of respect, *krishnāya*—to Krishna, *govindāya*—to Govinda, the cowherd, *vallabhāya*—to Him who was loved, *gopījana*—by the *gopis*, *namah*—salutations.

241

Radha Krishna Mantra

ॐ श्रीराधाकृष्णाय नमः ॥

shrī-rādhā-krishnāya namah

Om! Salutations to Radha and Krishna.

shrī—term of respect, *rādhā-krishnāya*—to Krishna accompanied by Radha, *namah*—salutations.

Gopijana Vallabha Mantra

ॐ नमो गोपीजनवल्लभाभ्याम् ॥

om namo gopījana-vallabhābhyām

Om! Salutations to those two loved by the *gopis*.

namah—salutations, *vallabhābhyām*—to those two, Radha and Krishna, who were loved, *gopījana*—by the *gopis*.

Gopijana Vallabha Mantra from Padma Purana

ॐ गोपीजनवल्लभचरणान् शरणं प्रपद्ये ॥

om gopījana-vallabha-caranān sharanam prapadye

Om! I seek refuge at the feet of those two loved by the *gopis*.

prapadye—I seek, *sharanam*—refuge, *caranān*—at the feet, *vallabha*—of those two who were loved, *gopījana*—by the *gopis*.

Mantras for Rama, Sita, and Hanuman

Rama is an incarnation of Vishnu who is considered the embodiment of dharma, righteousness. Rama's dark color identifies Him as an incarnation of Vishnu. His bow represents infinite power and His right hand is held in *abhaya mudra*, a gesture assuring there is nothing to fear. Sita is His consort and represents the ideal wife. Hanuman is His servant, representing the ideal devotee.

Meditation Verse for Rama — *dhyāna shloka*

रामाय रामभद्राय रामचन्द्राय वेधसे ।
रघुनाथाय नाथाय सीतायाः पतये नमः ॥

rāmāya rāmabhadrāya rāmacandrāya vedhase
raghunāthāya nāthāya sītāyāh pataye namah

Salutations (*namah*) to Rama (*rāmāya*), to the holy Rama (*rāmabhadrāya*), to the beautiful Rama (*rāmacandrāya*), to Vishnu (*vedhase*), to the master (*nātha*) and head of the Raghu clan (*raghunāthāya*), to the husband (*pataye*) of Sita (*sītāyāh*).

Rama Mantra

ॐ श्रीरामाय नमः ॥

om shrī-rāmāya namah
Om! Salutations to Rama.

shrī—term of respect, *rāmāya*—to Rama, *namah*—salutations.

Rama Raksha Mantra

ॐ श्रीराम जय राम जय जय राम ॥

om shrī-rām jay rām jay jay rām
Om! Hail Rama.

shrī—term of respect, *rām*—O Rama, *jay*—hail.

Sita Rama Mantra

ॐ श्रीसीतारामचन्द्राभ्यां नमः ॥

om shrī-sitā-rāmacandrābhyam namah
Om! Salutations to Sita and Ramacandra.

shrī—term of respect, *sitā-rāmacandrābhyam*—to Sita and Ramacandra, *namah*—salutations.

Rama Sharana Mantra

ॐ श्रीरामः शरणं मम ॥

om shrī-rāmah sharanam mama
Om! Rama is my refuge.

shrī—term of respect, *rāmah*—Rama, *mama*—my, *sharanam*—refuge.

Ramacandra Mantra

ॐ श्रीरामचन्द्रचरणौ शरणं प्रपद्ये ॥

om shrī-rāmacandra-caranau sharanam

Om! I seek refuge at Rama's holy feet.

prapadye—I seek, *sharanam*—refuge, *caranau*—at the feet of,
shrī—term of respect, *rāmacandra*—Rama.

Hanuman Mantra

ॐ श्रीहनुमते नमः ॥

om shrī-hanumate namah

Om! Salutations to Hanuman.

shrī—term of respect, *hanumate*—to Hanuman, *namah*—
salutations.

Anjaneya Mantra

ॐ नमो भगवते आञ्जनेयाय महाबलाय स्वाहा ॥

om namo bhagavate ānjaneyāya mahābalāya svāhā

Om! Salutations to Bhagavan Hanuman,
the powerful son of Anjani. *Svāhā!*

namah—salutations, *bhagavate*—to Bhagavan, *ānjaneyāya*—to
the son of Anjani, *mahābalāya*—to the powerful one, *svāhā*—
mantra of offering.

Mantras for Shiva

In the Hindu trinity of creator-sustainer-destroyer, Shiva or Maheshvara is known as the destroyer. But Shiva is more correctly understood as *upasamhāra kartā* — the one to whom the universe returns when this cycle of creation comes to an end. For this reason, Shiva can also be considered the God of time, change, and transformation.

In many depictions, He holds a drum (*damaru*) and fire (*agni*) in His upper right and left hands, symbolizing creation and destruction respectively. In other depictions, He holds a trident (*trishula*) representing His control over the three fundamental qualities (*gunas*) of nature. His third eye represents the capacity to destroy evil and a snake draped around His body represents infinite power.

Meditation Verse for Shiva — *dhyāna shloka*

वन्दे शम्भुमुमापतिं सुरगुरुं वन्दे जगत्कारणं
वन्दे पन्नगभूषणं मृगधरं वन्दे पशूनां पतिम् ।
वन्दे सूर्यशशाङ्कवह्निनयनं वन्दे मुकुन्दप्रियं
वन्दे भक्तजनाश्रयं च वरदं वन्दे शिवं शङ्करम् ॥

vande shambhum umāpatim suragurum vande jagat-kāranam
vande pannaga-bhushanam mrigadharam vande pashūnām patim
vande sūrya-shashānka-vahni-nayanam vande mukunda-priyam
vande bhakta-janāshrayam ca varadam vande shivam shankaram

I worship (*vande*) Shiva Shambhu, husband (*pati*) of Parvati, guru of the gods (*sura*), cause (*kārana*) of the world (*jagat*), adorned (*bhushana*) with a snake (*pannaga*), holding (*dhara*) a deer (*mriga*), Lord (*pati*) of creatures (*pashūnām*), having the sun (*sūrya*), moon (*shashānka*), and fire (*vahni*) as eyes (*nayana*), loved (*priya*) by Krishna (*mukunda*), refuge (*āshraya*) for devotees (*bhakta-jana*), giver of boons (*varada*), and source of peace (*shankara*).

Shiva Mantra

ॐ नमः शिवाय ॥

om namah shivāya

Om! Salutations to Shiva.

namah—salutations, *shivāya*—to Shiva.

Rudra Mantra

ॐ नमो भगवते रुद्राय ॥

om namo bhagavate rudrāya

Om! Salutations to Bhagavan Rudra.

namah—salutations, *bhagavate*—to Bhagavan, *rudrāya*—to Rudra (a Vedic name for Shiva).

247

Shiva Gayatri

ॐ तत्पुरुषाय विद्महे महादेवाय धीमहि ।
तन्नो रुद्रः प्रचोदयात् ॥

*om tat-purushāya vidmahe mahādevāya dhīmahi
tan no rudrah pracodayāt*

We contemplate (*vidmahe*) upon that (*tat*) supreme being (*purushāya*), we meditate (*dhīmahi*) on Mahadeva (*mahādevāya*). That (*tat*) Rudra (*rudrah*), may He guide (*pracodayāt*) us (*nah*).

Mahamrityunjaya Mantra

ॐ त्र्यम्बकं यजामहे सुगन्धिं पुष्टिवर्धनम् ।
उर्वारुकमिव बन्धनान् मृत्योर्मुक्षीय मामृतात् ॥

*om tryambakam yajāmahe sugandhim pushti-vardhanam
urvārukam iva bandhanān mrityor mukshīya mā'mritāt*

We worship (*yajāmahe*) the three-eyed Shiva (*tryambaka*) who is fragrant with blessings (*sugandhi*) and nurturing (*pushti-vardhana*). Just like (*iva*) a fruit (*urvāruka*) falls from the vine, free us (*mukshīya*) from the bondage (*bandhanāt*) of death (*mrityoh*), but not (*mā*) from immortality (*amritāt*).

Dakshinamurti Mantra

ॐ श्रीदक्षिणामूर्तये नमः ॥

om shrī-dakshināmūrtaye namah
Om! Salutations to Dakshinamurti.

shrī—term of respect, *dakshināmūrtaye*—to Dakshinamurti, Shiva as the first guru and source of spiritual wisdom, *namah*—salutations.

Medha Dakshinamurti Mantra

ॐ नमो भगवते दक्षिणामूर्तये
महचं मेधां प्रज्ञां प्रयच्छ स्वाहा ॥

om namo bhagavate dakshināmūrtaye
mahyam medhām prajnām prayaccha svāhā
Om! Salutations to Bhagavan Dakshinamurti.
Grant me intelligence and wisdom. *Svāhā!*

namah—salutations, *bhagavate*—to Bhagavan, *dakshināmūrtaye*
—unto Dakshinamurti, Shiva as the first guru, *prayaccha*—please
give, *medhā*—intelligence, *prajnā*—wisdom, *mahyam*—unto me,
svāhā—mantra of offering.

Mantras for Durga, Lakshmi and Sarasvati

Durga or Parvati is the consort of Shiva and His source
of energy or *shakti*. In some depictions, She holds an array of
weapons, representing Her tremendous power. Her vehicle is a
mighty lion.

Lakshmi, the consort of Vishnu, is the goddess of wealth.
She represents all that is maternal and nurturing. Her upper
hands hold lotus flowers, symbolizing purity. Her lower left
hand with downturned fingers bestows blessings and fulfills

desires. Her lower right hand with upturned fingers gives assurance that there is nothing to fear.

Sarasvati, the consort of Brahma, is goddess of all forms of knowledge, including music and the arts. She plays a musical instrument, *vīna*. Her upper right hand holds a *mālā* representing spiritual practice and Her lower left hand holds a book representing knowledge.

Meditation Verse for Durga — *dhyāna shloka*

सर्वमङ्गलमाङ्गल्ये शिवे सर्वार्थसाधिके ।
शरण्ये त्र्यम्बके गौरि नारायणि नमोऽस्तु ते ॥

*sarva-mangala-māngalye shive sarvārtha-sādhike
sharanye tryambake gauri nārāyani namo 'stu te*

O Narayani, the most holy (*māngalye*) of all that is holy (*sarva-mangala*), sacred (*shive*) refuge (*sharanye*) and fulfiller (*sādhike*) of all desires (*sarva-artha*), fair complexioned (*gauri*) with three eyes (*tryambake*), salutations (*namah*) unto (*astu*) you (*te*).

Durga Mantra

ॐ श्रीदुर्गायै नमः ॥
om shrī-durgāyai namah
Om! Salutations to Durga.

shrī—term of respect, *durgāyai*—to Durga, *namah*—salutations.

Durga Mula Mantra

ॐ ह्रीं दुं दुर्गायै नमः ॥

om hrīm dum durgāyai namah

Om! Hrīm! Dum! Salutations to Durga.

hrīm—invocation of Parvati, *dum*—invocation of Durga, *durgāyai*—to Durga, *namah*—salutations.

Durga Narayani Mantra

ॐ ह्रीं दुं दुर्गां देवीं शरणमहं प्रपद्ये ॥

om hrīm dum durgām devīm sharanam aham prapadye

Om! Hrīm! Dum! I seek refuge in goddess Durga.

hrīm—invocation of Parvati, *dum*—invocation of Durga, *aham*—I, *prapadye*—seek, *sharanam*—refuge, *durgām*—in Durga, *devīm*—goddess.

Durga Gayatri

ॐ कात्यायनाय विद्महे कन्यकुमारि धीमहि ।
तन्नो दुर्गिः प्रचोदयात् ॥

om kātyāyanāya vidmahe kanya-kumāri dhīmahi
tan no durgih pracodayāt

We contemplate (*vidmahe*) upon Katyayani (*kātyāyanāya*), we meditate (*dhīmahi*) on Kanyakumari. That (*tat*) Durga (*durgih*), may She guide (*pracodayāt*) us (*nah*).

251

Shakti Mantra

ॐ श्रीं ह्रीं क्लीं महाशक्त्यै नमः ॥

om shrīm hrīm klīm mahāshaktyai namah

Om! Shrīm! Hrīm! Klīm! Salutations to Mahashakti.

shrīm hrīm klīm—invocations of goddess, *mahāshaktyai*—to Mahashakti, goddess as energy, *namah*—salutations.

Kali Mantra

ॐ श्रीकालिकायै नमः ॥

om shrī-kālikāyai namah

Om! Salutations to Kali.

shrī—term of respect, *kālikāyai*—to Kali, *namah*—salutations.

Meditation Verse for Lakshmi — *dhyāna shloka*

पद्मालयां पद्मकरां पद्मपत्रनिभेक्षणाम् ।
वन्दे पद्ममुखीं देवीं पद्मनाभप्रियामहम् ॥

padmālayām padma-karām padma-patra-nibheksanām
vande padma-mukhīm devīm padma-nābha-priyām aham

I (*aham*) worship (*vande*) the goddess (*devīm*) abiding on a lotus (*padmālayām*), holding a lotus (*padmakarām*), with lotus eyes (*padma-patra-nibheksanām*) and face (*padma-mukhīm*), and loved by Vishnu (*padma-nābha-priyām*).

Mahalakshmi Mantra

ॐ श्रीं महालक्ष्म्यै नमः ॥

om shrīm mahālakshmyai namah

Om! Shrīm! Salutations to Mahalakshmi.

shrīm—invocation of Lakshmi, *mahālakshmyai*—to Mahalakshmi, *namah*—salutations.

Mahalakshmi Prasida Mantra

ॐ श्रीं ह्रीं श्रीं कमले कमलालये प्रसीद प्रसीद
श्रीं ह्रीं श्रीं महालक्ष्म्यै नमः ॥

om shrīm hrīm shrīm kamale kamalālaye prasīda prasīda
shrīm hrīm shrīm mahālakshmyai namah

Om! Shrīm! Hrīm! Shrīm! O goddess of the Lotus, be pleased.
Shrīm! Hrīm! Shrīm! Salutations to Mahalakshmi.

shrīm hrīm—invocations of goddess, *kamale*—O goddess of the lotus, *kamalālaye*—residing on a lotus, *prasīda*—be pleased, *mahālakshmyai*—unto Mahalakshmi, *namah*—salutations.

Lakshmi Gayatri

ॐ महादेव्यै च विद्महे विष्णुपत्न्यै च धीमहि ।
तन्नो लक्ष्मीः प्रचोदयात् ॥

om mahā-devyai ca vidmahe vishnu-patnyai ca dhīmahi
tan no lakshmīh pracodayāt

Om! We contemplate upon Mahadevi, we meditate on
Vishnu's wife. May Lakshmi guide us.

253

We contemplate (*vidmahe*) upon Mahadevi (*mahā-devyai*), we meditate (*dhīmahi*) on the wife of Vishnu (*vishnu-patnyai*). That (*tat*) Lakshmi (*lakshmīh*), may She guide (*pracodayāt*) us (*nah*).

Meditation Verse for Sarasvati—*dhyāna shloka*

या कुन्देन्दुतुषारहारधवला या शुभ्रवस्त्रावृता
या वीणावरदण्डमण्डितकरा या श्वेतपद्मासना ।
या ब्रह्माच्युतशङ्करप्रभृतिभिर्देवैस्सदा पूजिता
सा मां पातु सरस्वती भगवती निश्शेषजाड्यापहा ॥

yā kundendu-tushāra-hāra-dhavalā yā shubhra-vastrāvritā
yā vīnā-vara-danda-manditakarā yā shveta-padmāsanā
yā brahmācyuta-shankara-prabhritibhir devais sadā pūjitā
sā mām pātu sarasvatī bhagavatī nishshesha-jādyāpahā

Who (*yā*) is as fair (*dhavalā*) as a jasmine flower (*kunda*), the moon (*indu*), or snow (*tushāra-hāra*), dressed (*vastrāvritā*) in white (*shubhra*), whose hands hold (*manditakarā*) a veena (*vīnā-vara-danda*), sitting (*āsana*) on a white (*shveta*) lotus (*padmā*), always (*sadā*) worshiped (*pūjitā*) by Gods (*devaih*) like (*prabhritibhih*) Brahma, Vishnu (*acyuta*) and Shiva (*shankara*), remover (*apahā*) of all (*nishshesha*) ignorance (*jādyā*), may She (*sā*), goddess (*bhagavatī*) Sarasvati, protect (*pātu*) me (*mām*).

Sarasvati Mantra

ॐ ऐं सरस्वत्यै नमः ॥

om aim sarasvatyai namah
Om! Salutations to Sarasvati.

aim—invocation of Sarasvati, *sarasvatyai*—to Sarasvati, *namah*—salutations.

Miscellaneous Mantras

Mantra for Gratitude (see Exercise 7-2)

धन्योऽहं धन्योऽहं धन्योऽहं अहं धन्यः ॥

dhanyo'ham dhanyo'ham dhanyo'ham aham dhanyah
Blessed am I, blessed am I, blessed am I, I am blessed!

dhanyah—blessed, *aham*—I.

Ishvara Mantra

ॐ ईशाय नमः ॥

om īshāya namah
Om! Salutations to Ishvara.

īshāya—to Isha or Ishvara, *namah*—salutations.

So'ham Mantra (see Exercise 2-5)

सोऽहम् ॥

so 'ham
sah—that, *aham*—I. I am that (inner divinity).

Blessing for All (see Exercise 7-1)

लोकाः समस्ताः सुखिनो भवन्तु ॥
lokās samastās sukhino bhavantu
May all people be happy.

samastās—all, *lokās*—people, *bhavantu*—may they be, *sukhinah*
—happy.

Paramatma Mantra

ॐ परमात्मने नमः ॥
om paramātmane namah
Om! Salutations to Paramatma.

paramātmane—to Paramatma, the supreme self, *namah*—
salutations.

Parameshvara Mantra

ॐ परमेश्वराय नमः ॥
om parameshvarāya namah
Om! Salutations to Parameshvara.

parameshvarāya—to Parameshvara, the supreme Lord, *namah*—
salutations

Shanti Mantra

ॐ शान्तिः शान्तिः शान्तिः ॥
om shāntih shāntih shāntih
Om! Peace, peace, peace.

APPENDIX B

ONLINE RESOURCES

Swami Tadatmananda's ashram, Arsha Bodha Center, maintains a website to make his teachings on Vedanta, meditation, Bhagavad Gita, and other topics readily available.

The website includes a section dedicated to this book. It provides a variety of audio files you can freely listen to or download. The files include instructions for proper pronunciation and intonation of every mantra in Appendix A, as well as recordings of selected meditation exercises in this book. Also included are recordings of meditation programs conducted by Swami Tadatmananda at his ashram.

The website is www.arshabodha.org. Follow these links: Teachings > Meditation Book.

This book and other publications by Swami Tadatmananda are available on the website's bookstore.

ABOUT THE AUTHOR

Swami Tadatmananda was born in 1953 in Milwaukee, Wisconsin. After receiving a degree in electrical engineering, he worked in California where he found the opportunity to practice meditation and yoga under the guidance of several teachers from India. In 1981, he met Swami Dayananda, a traditional teacher of Vedanta.

He studied Vedanta and Sanskrit under Swami Dayananda's tutelage and went to India for further studies in 1986. He then left his home and profession to move to Arsha Vidya Gurukulam, an ashram in Pennsylvania's Pocono mountains, to undertake a three-year residential course in Vedanta, meditation, and Sanskrit taught by Swami Dayananda.

Soon after the course, Swami Tadatmananda assumed responsibility for managing Arsha Vidya Gurukulam. In 1993, he was initiated as a *sannyasi*, a Hindu monk, by Swami Dayananda on the banks of the Ganges River in Rishikesh. He then began to teach at Arsha Vidya Gurukulam and throughout the United States, giving lectures, seminars, and meditation workshops for various organizations, temples, universities, and industries.

In 2000, with the blessings of his guru, Swami Tadatmananda established his own ashram, Arsha Bodha Center in Somerset, New Jersey, where he continues to teach.

Swami Tadatmananda
Arsha Bodha Center
84 Cortelyous Lane
Somerset, NJ 08873
732-940-4008
www.arshabodha.org
SwamiT@arshabodha.org

BOOKS OF RELATED INTEREST

 **INNER GUIDE MEDITATION:** *A Spiritual Technology for the 21st Century* by Edwin Steinbrecher

ISBN: 0604

 **KARMA AND CHAOS:** *by Paul R. Fleischman, Forrest D. Fleischman*

ISBN: 1772

 **MEDITATION GUIDEBOOK:** *Practice and Application by Jose Lorenzo-Fuentes*

ISBN: 1779

 **MEDITATIONS FOR PEOPLE IN CHARGE** *by Paul Brunton*

ISBN: 3452

 **MEDITATIONS FOR PEOPLE IN CRISIS** *by Paul Brunton, Sam Cohen, Leslie Cohen*

ISBN: 3414

 **THE ORIGIN OF MEDITATION** *by Sneh Chakraburtty*

ISBN: 3230

 **THE SCIENCE OF MEDITATION** *by Sneh Chakraburtty*

ISBN: 3223

 **THE STORY OF MEDITATION** *by Sneh Chakraburtty*

ISBN: 3216